Brief Counseling
with RET

Brief Counseling with RET

Paul A. Hauck

The Westminster Press
Philadelphia

First edition

Published by The Westminster Press ®
Philadelphia, Pennsylvania

PRINTED IN THE UNITED STATES OF AMERICA

9 8 7 6 5 4 3 2 1

Library of Congress Cataloging in Publication Data

Hauck, Paul A
  Brief counseling with RET

  Bibliography: p.
  1. Rational-emotive psychotherapy. 2. Psychotherapy, Brief. 3. Counseling. I. Title.
RC489.R3H38   616.89'14   80–10377
ISBN 0–664–24314–2

Contents

Preface

I am fifty-four years old and have been practicing clinical psychology for twenty-five years. At the time I began my career Freud and psychoanalysis were the popular subjects at the universities throughout the country. Textbooks on testing, on the theory of psychopathology, and on the techniques of therapy were few. A clinical psychologist had no assurance twenty-five years ago that he would ever be employed to practice therapy. If you want an example of a motivation killer, there you have one. Can you guess how much drive a student had to have for a field of study which was so poorly defined that it had no firm policy statement regarding counseling?

I guess I was more stubborn than practical. I simply plowed ahead for the Ph.D. because I didn't know what else to do. When I accepted my first position in Butte, Montana, I was unprepared. By today's standards I was a complete beginner, Ph.D. or no. I sincerely hope no one these days ever goes into the field with as poor preparation as I and other colleagues had.

I have had to learn the hard way, and in the process of developing my clinical skills I have sometimes had to be a pioneer and lead the way through a jungle of ignorance. This has been a challenge all the way. As such, it has been an interesting journey but often a tough one.

Brief therapy was one of those areas of concern that was

most wanting back in those green years. Psychoanalysis was totally unsuited to the needs of an adolescent boy who was depressed over rejection by his sweetheart. He needed help now, not after spilling his heart out for a few years.

Franz Alexander was one of the first disciples of Freud to pay attention to short-term therapy (Alexander and Ross, 1952). His ideas were interesting and worked reasonably well in some instances. His contributions were limited, however, because he was still working within the framework of psychoanalytic concepts, such as transference, repetition compulsion, and oedipal fixations. He is to be remembered fondly, however, because he recognized how impractical his psychoanalytic teachings were as a rapid therapeutic tool, and offered psychoanalytically-oriented psychotherapy as an answer to this need.

Carl Rogers next took the transference phenomenon completely out of serious consideration in therapy (Rogers, 1951, 1961). He also promised a quicker result. So I naturally learned what I could of his teachings and gave them a try. To my delight a few of my more verbal clients who were also given to introspection put two and two together and came up with four. However, the range of applicability of the nondirective method was soon apparent and I looked for greener pastures. About the only remnants of those early teachings I still take seriously are his insistence that having a high positive regard for the client helps therapy and that when the therapist keeps quiet long enough for the client to talk without fear of criticism or interruption, valuable facts and feelings get expressed. I haven't forgotten those two points.

So I stumbled along and almost decided to become a shoe salesman, when I tried Gestalt therapy for a time. It too had its fascinating features, but I found it limited in application to the vast range of problems in a community mental health center or a private practice.

Then in 1964 I planned to attend a postdoctoral institute at Temple University in Philadelphia. The leader of the four-day workshop developed heart trouble weeks before the meeting. Those who signed up for his seminar were asked to select other classes. I chose a workshop on rational-emotive therapy to be given by Albert Ellis. My life has not been the same since.

Since that course in Philadelphia my therapeutic technique is a combination of all the methods I have known. However, the foundation rock, the substratum on which my therapeutic efforts rest, is practically always the principles of RET (Rational-Emotive Therapy). Though I may stray from a true RET course during any particular counseling session, I find myself comfortable only when the basics of RET have been faithfully observed in the long run.

Soon I discovered that I could give myself therapy quite easily. This I found to be truly remarkable. Many times in the previous years I had tried being my own therapist when I became depressed or tense. Giving myself therapy for anger didn't even occur to me. At that time, ventilation of hostility was looked upon as healthy, not neurotic. And of course I was not able to help myself at all with a series of nightmares I went through during one week of my life some months prior to the workshop at Temple University.

RET has been my method for personal therapy ever since those days of first discovery. My depressions have almost completely vanished. I suffer only the mildest pangs of guilt, and no inferiority at all. My angers have been brief and not intense. I have worried a bit when serious issues arose but when confronting everyday annoyances I have talked myself out of catastrophizing hundreds of times.

And what about self-discipline? I've always had pretty good control of myself, but with RET that has improved too. Without the knowledge of how to get tasks accomplished I would never have been able to develop a thriving practice, have two or three consultations going most of the time, write nine books, and enjoy tennis, skiing, and jogging as part of a wider physical fitness program.

I am writing this in the hallway of a courthouse as I wait to be called to appear as an expert witness in court. In moments like this, my book will be completed. To have a whole twelve months to write a book would be like slow death. To have a few moments here and there is like snacking from a large box of candies—never so much to become satiated, always just enough to whet the appetite.

RET, your secrets are divine. But perhaps your greatest charm is this ability to provide us with self-help. It's extremely comforting to me to know that I can be on an airplane and talk myself out of a tense reaction as the plane lurches. Or if I find myself on a dark street, on a distant Canadian lake, or shooting along an interstate expressway, I can be my own therapist and keep myself calm. Try doing that sometime without having your analyst along.

RET conceives of therapy mainly as a matter of education. We are psychologically distressed because we lack knowledge. When we become educated to the causes and the relief of emotional distress we are finally able to control our mental well-being. This is a crucial point to grasp if you wish to practice brief counseling with RET.

Think of this method as something that affects your clients because you teach them the psychological facts of life. Think of yourself not so much as a therapist but as a teacher. You give lessons in your classroom, not treatment in a clinic or an office. You don't treat people, you educate them. They are often not sick, just ignorant (Szasz, 1961). Just as in school you expect homework, textbooks, and lectures, that is what you can expect from RET. That's why I write books, make tapes, and give seminars, workshops, and lectures. That's why other RET therapists do the same. To conduct brief therapy with RET you may think of yourself as an educator who will spend much therapeutic time asking questions, giving advice, and debating vigorously with your students when they don't accept your counsel (Ellis, 1962).

Is this playing God? Hardly. Is your piano teacher playing God when she corrects your fingering while you attempt to master a run? Is your coach a conceited person when he tells you how to cut a wide curve to receive a pass? Is your shop teacher conceited when he warns you the wood had better be sanded after it is stained? Is your math teacher being unreasonable when she corrects your algebra answer?

The point is, you're the expert in your office. If you don't feel qualified, get more instruction until you're sure you know your subject matter. It's difficult to teach a subject if you haven't mastered it yourself.

When you have learned your material and you can use it on yourself, then, and only then, are you in a position to help others expertly. The help you give before you attain that state of expertise makes you prone to the usual errors all inexperienced professionals will endure. Do so nevertheless. The sooner you start, the sooner you learn. But remember this: you have knowledge, you have answers, and you are often right. The client, by virtue of talking to you, is not right, and does not know what you know, because he or she is disturbed, confused, or self-defeating. You, in the main, are not.

This is not conceit. It is reality. Conceit is an issue only when you regard yourself better than your client and superior as a human being, merely because you are more knowledgeable in the field of psychology. You are better informed, to be sure, but you are not a better human, only a better counselor.

Those who are unfamiliar with RET will find sufficient instruction in this book to take it up satisfactorily if you have experience as a counselor already. Try it, gingerly at first, by taking a more directive part with one or two clients. Instead of reflecting sentiments with your next depressed self-pitier, try getting the client to stop feeling sorry for himself or herself. The next time you encounter a hostile husband, a banshee of a wife, or a brat of a teenager, instead of sympathetically listening to their childish complaints and demands, tell them off for a change. Teach them that it isn't necessary to flip one's lid and that all anger is a sign of grandiosity.

You'll probably find yourself trying to handle other problems with RET. Soon you'll notice that you are getting results so much faster and with a sense of comprehension as to why you are getting changes that you'll probably never go back to your former school of thought.

If you are an experienced therapist, this book will be invaluable to you as a guide to the best principles of practicing RET. Get your supervised training along with the study of this book and join a new group of contented therapists who are making an impact on emotional problems not possible until now.

Let me close this Preface with an example of brief therapy. This case epitomizes the best techniques from RET: education and homework assignments.

The client should have been flying over the Atlantic on his way to Europe. Instead, he was in my office, pacing back and forth like a caged tiger. His company had offered him a new assignment with a considerable increase in responsibility. Naturally, I thought he might have been uneasy about taking over a difficult project. He wasn't. However, he did mention that he expected opposition from some of the managers already in Europe. This was discussed, but he felt it was not so unpleasant a prospect as to cause him to be this tense.

Was he afraid of flying? No. He had flown often and never had such a reaction. Then why was he upset? We couldn't detect it in the first thirty-minute session on Monday.

I had made tapes on RET, and sent him home with several, asking him to listen to them carefully to see if they gave any clues as to how he was upsetting himself.

He came back the following day with several suggestions as to what could be distressing him. None made much sense. I tried hypnotizing him to give symptomatic relief, but this did not work either. He was getting more tense and depressed as he realized how far off schedule he was. I sent him home with my book *Overcoming Depression,* hoping he could determine what was troubling him and perhaps get some relief.

He returned Wednesday with a few suggestions as to the cause of his distress. One of them made sense: that he might eat, drink, and smoke to excess while batching it in Europe. He had recently been given a physical examination and was told to lose weight and to stop smoking completely. This was being accomplished, until a couple of weeks prior to his scheduled flight. Then he began smoking again, lightly this time. His wife, however, chided him for his lax discipline and he regained control easily.

Suddenly everything fell into place. He was afraid that he would slip into unhealthy habits if his wife was not along to help him control them. He strongly felt that when on his own he was sure to dissipate and seriously injure his health.

The remainder of the hour-long session on Wednesday was pure RET. I pointed out that he was catastrophizing over the possibility of starting a bad habit. What if he did? Certainly it could kill him. So could the plane flight to Europe. And since when couldn't he discipline himself again? Did he really need a mama along to scold him into proper conduct, he who had shown brilliant advancement in his company, he who had shown fantastic self-discipline for years as he worked his way up the corporate ladder? I couldn't buy that for a minute, and we disputed this actively until he calmed down when he realized he had foolishly made a mountain out of a pack of cigarettes or a few steins of beer.

I later learned he took off quite comfortably Thursday morning and was probably flying over the Atlantic as his wife was giving me the news over the phone.

I was pleased that they were pleased. But I was most pleased with the tools and techniques I was able to bring to this problem. Before my RET days, that gentleman would have been sitting in my office for weeks while his career dreams evaporated.

So this book is about brief counseling and the RET principles that make it possible. I hope it works for you as well as it has for me.

P.A.H.

Acknowledgment

After being my personal secretary for over ten years, Mrs. Gladys Leach is retiring. It was she who typed most of my books, who put herself out to squeeze the manuscript typing in between her other duties, and who always did a professional job. I am enormously grateful to her for her loyalty and skill.

Thanks.

— P.A.H.

Chapter 1

The Fundamentals of RET

Quite simply, RET takes the position that practically all emotional problems are created in our heads (Ellis, 1961, 1962, 1966). When we think about problems in an alarming, angry, or depressed way, we feel alarmed, angry, or depressed. That does not have to happen if we would alter our self-talk. It is the way we think of things that upsets us, not the events themselves. Epictetus, the Greek scholar, knew this thousands of years ago. (Hadas, 1962). Marcus Aurelius, the Roman emperor, wrote a manual for the Roman soldiers so that they could endure great distress with equanimity. That politician knew more psychology than a lot of the therapists do today. Read his Meditations (Marcus Aurelius, 1900) or go to Epictetus' Enchiridion (Epictetus, 1899), and you will see the cornerstone of modern RET unfold before your eyes. Shakespeare also perceived the incredible role our thoughts have over our feelings. "It is our opinions of things which distress us, not the things themselves." Even Sigmund Freud conceded that the voice of the intellect, though soft, had a powerful influence over our feelings (Freud, 1945). And finally, from the Bible in Phil. 4:11 we have the same theme: "Not that I speak in respect of want: for I have learned, in whatsoever state I am, therewith to be content."

If these thoughts on psychological wisdom have been around so long, why did it take the world so long to employ them in therapy? Because Freud had a powerful influence over our thinking in psychopathology for decades, asking that we repeatedly search out what happened in the client's past rather than what he was saying to himself in the present (Freud, 1935, 1938).

Before Freud, there were centuries during which human behavior was viewed as controlled by demons and Satan. Epictetus was largely forgotten until his thoughts were focused on again by the founder of the RET school of thought: Albert Ellis. It is essential to become acquainted in detail with the theory of RET.

THE THEORY OF RET

Pain arises from two sources: (1) internal or external agents that can act directly upon flesh and bone, and (2) thoughts. The first kind of pain comes from being struck, shoved, hit, frozen, starved, etc. The second comes from thinking irrationally. In greater detail the theory can be explained as follows (Ellis, 1957, 1961, 1962, 1966, 1972):

Let A stand for an activating event. This can be any form of human behavior. If A is a physical event and causes pain, that is, if there is a direct connection between the event and the pain, then we can justifiably say that A causes C, the consequences.

For example, if A (a baseball) hits you on the head and causes C (a painful bump), it is correct to conclude that A caused C. There is no dispute over this issue. How can there be?

But wait, controversy arises quickly as soon as A—the activating event—is a thought. People have for centuries believed that a gesture, a smile, or a profanity can hurt us in the same way a smack on the mouth or a bullet can. For them, A (someone's unkind or unflattering behavior) can also cause C (the pain).

This time, however, we are dealing with a psychological, an emotional pain (depression, anger, or worry). This pain (C) is not caused by A but by our interpretation of A, our opinion of A, what we tell ourselves about A. Let's call this mental process B.

B causes our emotional difficulties. B represents the opinions Shakespeare referred to when he said, "It is our opinions of things which distress us, not the things themselves." This statement can be rewritten as follows: B causes C, A does not, *if* C is a psychological pain.

This means that you do not *directly* upset anyone. You may provide the frustrations over which others *elect* to upset themselves, but that is not your responsibility, it is *theirs*. The only exceptions to this rule are in the cases of children, mental defectives, or those who can no longer think logically, such as those who are senile.

You may protest at this point that surely many events of a psychological nature are so stressful that people *must* become seriously upset over them. What about death, desertion, divorce, unfair treatment, and a host of other cruel acts?

A close study of human behavior invariably reveals that people react to such stresses in a variety of ways, not just one (Anderson, 1966; Arieti, 1959). Some persons accept divorce with a reasonable degree of sadness, while others commit suicide. In either case the blow is no more cruel in one instance than in another. How to account for the difference? The difference is B again, the way people view the frustration. If they feel disappointed over the divorce, they will feel sad. This is a normal and not unhealthy response to stress. However, becoming mightily upset to the point of immobility and great psychic pain is unhealthy.

If the happenings in our lives actually had a *direct* relationship to our emotions, we would all feel *almost* the same after being rejected, after failing, or after a great disappointment. Such is the case with physical events. If the temperature drops fifty degrees, we all feel colder. If we cut our food intake in half, we all lose weight. And persons with similar physical conditioning double up with a pain if punched in the stomach.

But when the pain is an *indirect* result of our thinking

rather than a direct effect on our physical beings, we encounter a great variety of responses. These responses depend on how casually or seriously we view events. Certainly everyone who is rained on at a picnic will get wet, but not all will be upset. Some will be saddened, some gladdened, and some furious. Yet the rain is the same for all. In greater detail, the process goes as follows.

When people talk to themselves at B (the Belief System), they express two kinds of thoughts: rational beliefs (rB) and irrational beliefs (iB). The rational beliefs are causing no pain, but the irrational ones are. The latter are often difficult for disturbed clients to detect. These clients naturally think they are making good sense and they haven't the slightest idea at times how they are distressing themselves with their foolish thinking.

For instance, a young man whom you want to counsel over his anger may not be able to realize how he is making himself angry after his car fender was dented in an accident caused solely by the other driver.

You ask him to tell you what he is telling himself about the accident which could be making him angry and all you get are a string of rational beliefs (rB's):

1. It's going to cost a lot of money to repair the fender. (True: rB)
2. My insurance rates may go up. (True: rB)
3. This accident could have easily been avoided if the other driver had not been lighting a cigarette. (True: rB)
4. My employer may fire me when he finds out I've been in another accident. (True: rB)
5. My license may be revoked. (True: rB)
6. And so on and on and on.

The extremely important point to bear in mind, however, is that *not one* of these rational beliefs (rB's) explains the young man's distress. He is making sense with each one of these views. His thinking is logical, correct, and beyond reproach. That's why these beliefs do not upset him. Rational thinking is free of pain. A rational driver will become *unhappy* over the consequences he envisions, he will be *annoyed* and *put out,* but he will not go into a tailspin and become whining, or violent, or suicidal. He will not think the other driver is a villain who deserves to be thrashed, or that his life is ruined forever, or that he has been disgraced.

The driver who becomes *neurotic* over the accident has expressed one or more *irrational beliefs* to himself. If we are to help him remain calm, it is imperative that we: *(a)* seek out those irrational beliefs, *(b)* communicate them to the client, *(c)* show him *why* they are irrational, *(d)* and instruct him to debate with himself as to why his so-called "rational beliefs" are actually very irrational.

If need be, we can take his rational beliefs step by step and demonstrate to him how he has followed his rB's with iB's. This brings us to the next step in the ABC theory. D stands for Disputing the irrational ideas. The disputing begins with you, the counselor, showing the client which irrational ideas he has and why they are irrational.

Back to our angry client. His first rational belief was, "It's going to cost a lot of money to repair the fender."

The irrational beliefs that could follow that sane thought are: "It's unfair that it should cost so much to fix a small dent. Auto makers should make cars so that repair bills are much smaller. It's terrible to have to live with all this unfairness."

These thoughts are irrational, because it is not objectively true that small dents should cost little. Who says so? Auto makers have every right to construct cars that look beautiful and sleek but that cost like mad when they need repairs.

Furthermore, it is not terrible to live with all that unfairness, it is merely regrettable. Does your client not have another car? Does he not have a roof over his head? Does the home not have central heating and air conditioning? Does he not enjoy good health, have a secure job, belong to a happy family, and live in a society that makes life remarkably comfortable for him? Of course he does.

Then what's so terrible? Just because a sad and imperfect occurrence takes place in his life, is he seriously trying to tell us that his life has become unbearable because he is unfairly being penalized for an accident he did not cause?

His second rational belief, "My insurance rates will go up," may be true (rB), but that is hardly the end of the world (iB).

The third rational belief, that the accident could easily have been avoided (rB), should not be followed by the thought, "Therefore it *should not* have happened." Why not? Since when don't imperfect things happen in an imperfect world? And why does he have to get upset just because he's not getting his way? Who said he ran the world anyway?

After you have taught your client to Dispute the irrational ideas, he will experience new Effects. At first he will gain an intellectual or cognitive understanding of his problem (cE), followed by a behavioral Effect (bE). The cognitive Effect results from thinking through prior neurotic philosophies and seeing them as erroneous. When, for example, we can truly appreciate the fact that we are not perfect human beings and will behave badly from time to time, we have gained a cognitive Effect. When we honestly understand that any wicked act we or others perform is the result of deficiency, ignorance, or emotional disturbance, and that we have a perfect right to forgive ourselves or anyone else completely for any act, no matter how cruel, bizarre, or stupid, we have arrived at a cognitive restructuring of our view of people and the world.

The more cognitive Effects we achieve, the more our thinking becomes rational and sane and the more undisturbed we will feel. That's where the last step comes in (bE). The behavioral Effect is the way we feel as a result of our changed thinking. Instead of blaming ourselves over a misdeed, we accept that error as part of our imperfection and proceed to focus on it to bring about a change. We won't be pleased with our cruel behavior, but we won't crucify ourselves over it either. Instead, after reaching a condition of relative tranquillity by disputing the irrational ideas behind the disturbance, we will be in an excellent position to take stock of our behavior and rationally do something about it. With bE the disturbance is over, we feel better, happier, and more confident.

TWELVE IRRATIONAL IDEAS

The thoughts that create our disturbances have been carefully studied by Albert Ellis, Ph.D., the originator of RET. He found that there are eleven irrational ideas (Ellis, 1962). In 1978, Ellis modified his eleven irrational ideas and expanded them by one. Some years ago I offered a twelfth (Hauck, 1972). To understand how your client gets upset, you can review the following list of irrational ideas and discover which ones apply. This list, which is the cornerstone of RET, should be mastered by the counselor. The irrational ideas do not need to be learned word for word or by number. It is extremely helpful, however, to become so familiar with them that you can easily associate a particular emotion with the one or more irrational ideas usually responsible for it. I will go into this point more fully later. For now, here are the twelve irrational ideas with explanations of their irrationality. (Adapted from Paul A. Hauck, *Reason in Pastoral Counseling,* pp. 31–51; Westminster Press, 1972.)

IRRATIONAL IDEA NO. 1: "The idea that it is a dire necessity for an adult human being to be loved or approved by virtually every significant other person in the community." (The word "adult" should be particularly noted.)

This is a foolish notion for the simple reason that another person's evaluation of us is always determined by that person's own personality quirks. The person is seldom the authority about us that we ourselves are, and probably is also suffering under this irrational idea and may therefore feel worthless unless our approval is given or the approval of someone whom the person greatly respects.

IRRATIONAL IDEA NO. 2: "The idea that one should be thoroughly competent, adequate, and achieving in all possible respects if one is to consider oneself worthwhile."

Our achievements do not reflect upon our worthiness, only upon our talents and experiences. The man who runs the mile under four minutes is not a better person, he is only a better runner. To judge ourselves by our behavior puts an intolerable burden upon us to be perfect. One is either perfect or one is bad, wicked, and evil.

The suffering that this idea of achieved worth has caused is impossible to estimate. Why not simply avoid this emotional detour and get right on to the correcting of the problem? By overthrowing Irrational Idea No. 2 we can do this.

IRRATIONAL IDEA NO. 3: "The idea that certain people are bad, wicked, or villainous and that they should be severely blamed and punished for their villainy."

Blame is here defined as a criticism of and anger over a person's unacceptable behavior and the person as well. It is totally logical to think of behavior as wicked, and the person committing it as acceptable. Wrong deeds are committed for at least one of three very good reasons. (1) One may not know right from wrong. If Tom, a twenty-year-old mental defective, carelessly drops his cigarette in a farmer's barn causing it to burn to the ground, we can hardly consider him a villain despite his tragic and costly act. *He* is not bad, although his *behavior* was. (2) Ignorance is the second reason why people frequently commit wrong deeds. Had they better skills, greater ability, or more thorough training, they would surely not act in the erroneous fashion they do. The adolescent who shoots his hunting companion by mistake is not an evil person although his act is fatal. Perhaps he did not have knowledge of the safety catch or how to carry his weapon. Can he be blamed for something he does not know? (3) The third reason people behave badly is their neurotic personalities. They have been taught by an irrational society to think and behave in self-defeating ways. The amnesiac who deserts his family has never been taught full responsibility and the technique whereby he can carry his burdens with equanimity. The murderer is also not wicked although his act is. He too lacks the training required to handle problems by better means. He is not evil but disturbed, neurotic, infantile, etc. This, of course, does not relieve him of the responsibility for his acts. He committed the acts and had better suffer the consequences. But it makes no sense to blame him for his shortcomings. In the majority of cases this only serves to make him hate himself and then feel unable to behave better.

IRRATIONAL IDEA NO. 4: "The idea that it is awful and catastrophic when things are not the way one would very much like them to be."

Rather than create disturbances within ourselves over the events of the world, we can try to change, prevent, or modify these events. Those events which cannot now, or ever, be changed, can be accepted philosophically instead of resentfully.

IRRATIONAL IDEA NO. 5: "The idea that human unhappiness is externally caused and that people have little or no ability to control their sorrows and disturbances."

This idea is irrational because it ignores the vital distinction between a frustration and a disturbance. The fact that one practically always follows the other does not vouch for its validity. A mother will be mightily upset at her child's messiness one day and ignore the same state of affairs the next. If the messiness really had the power to disturb her, it would do so both days.

IRRATIONAL IDEA NO. 6: "The idea that if something is or may be dangerous or fearsome one should be terribly concerned about it and should keep dwelling on the possibility of its occurring."

Many persons think worry is essential to the eventual solution of their problems. They believe they must feel anxiety over their problems if they are to attack them seriously.

The worrier, burdened with needless anxiety and fear, actually often compounds a problem. An adolescent who has had one automobile accident can precipitate another by becoming nervous.

IRRATIONAL IDEA NO. 7: "The idea that it is easier to avoid than to face certain life difficulties and self-responsibilities."

As obvious as this may sound, it is astonishing how many people do not accept this thought as being irrational. To be sure, it is readily accepted intellectually as foolish, but it is a problem to us all. People who avoid facing their problems to buy a moment's relief pay enormously in later frustration and pain for those fleeting snatches of well-being. Relief is never lasting if we follow this belief.

IRRATIONAL IDEA NO. 8: "The idea that one should be dependent on others and needs someone stronger than oneself on whom to rely."

Excessive dependency stems from two sources: lack of self-confidence and the belief that failure proves one's worthlessness. Relying too much on other persons tends to perpetuate both conditions. Confidence comes to us only when we have individually accomplished some task. Much learning is trial and error. The trial phase in this process is omitted when others try for us.

IRRATIONAL IDEA NO. 9: "The idea that one's past history is an all-important determiner of one's present behavior and that because something once strongly affected one's life, it should indefinitely have a similar effect."

This philosophy works dangerously against persons in counseling. It has entered into society from psychoanalysis which has repeatedly emphasized the influence of childhood on our adult lives. While these findings cannot be totally refuted, the interpretation that change is impossible unless many childhood memories are revived must be denied.

IRRATIONAL IDEA NO. 10: "The idea that one should become quite upset over other people's problems and disturbances."

To incur an ulcer or a depression in an attempt to change another individual is folly. Such results are as bad or worse than a disease. The price for change is too great if it entails emotional disturbance. One disturbance has a way of breeding another until other areas of the relationship are also in jeopardy.

IRRATIONAL IDEA NO. 11: "The idea that there is invariably a right, precise, and perfect solution to human problems and that it is catastrophic if this perfect solution is not found."

Only death is certain. To delay a decision because it does not satisfy us totally is a demand for certainty. Normally, problems have several possible solutions, none of which may strike us as ideal. Still, it is far better to initiate *some* action than to take none at all. Reason and negative emotions cannot operate simultaneously. Either we are thinking clearly (and remain calm) or we are thinking foolishly (and become disturbed). Reason and disturbance do not coexist. At the same moment one cannot think wisely and unwisely.

IRRATIONAL IDEA NO. 12: The idea that beliefs held by respected authorities or society must be correct and should not be questioned.

The idea is irrational for the following reasons:
1. It presumes that one is capable of perfection, a condition no thinking person can support. Any authority, be it a person or a social institution, has only limited wisdom and

through long periods of time often comes to view yesterday's "truths" as today's errors. Wisdom is obtained through the accretion of experience and the erosion of beliefs that do not stand the test of reason. No matter how slowly, practically all beliefs and ideas undergo modification.

2. The very "truths" that the neurotic person fears to question were themselves the product of a previous disbelief.

3. Deciding which authority or which society a person will accept is more often an accident of birth, location, and time than it is the result of careful study. "Authoritative" views of widely divergent natures are almost always held by others if one will but explore far enough. To accept one authority is to deny another.

Rather than regard beliefs as eternal truths held by infallible individuals or institutions, a more rational approach would consider these points:

Institutions such as governments, universities, and churches are the product of human effort. Since all humans are imperfect and error-prone, so are their institutions. The final truth, therefore, cannot be the province of any person or group of persons.

Truth, as scientifically conceived, is always incomplete and is arrived at through controlled trial and error.

Very few thinkers have been able to influence generations long after their deaths. Most respected sages have only momentary recognition and are soon forgotten. Since one cannot know how one's mentor will fare in the pages of history, one is wisest always to have reservations about the mentor's teachings.

THE GOALS OF BRIEF THERAPY

First, arbitrarily I define brief therapy as a dozen or fewer sessions. The time period can extend from one to twelve consecutive days or one to twelve visits stretched out over a twelve-month period. The briefness refers to the time required of the therapist, not of the client.

People behave in four broad emotional styles. These are

typical patterns of balance between feelings of euphoria, pleasure, and goodwill, and pain, discontentment, and neurotic self-defeatism.

The first pattern is the typical mood swing commonly observed in the manic-depressive. If one were to draw a line across this page that signified a degree of neutrality between pleasure and pain, persons with mood swings would have a curve like a mountain for the first part, followed by a valley for the second part, followed by another rounded mountain, and so on, like this:

Emotional Style No. 1

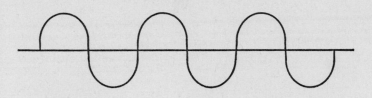

The second typical pain-pleasure curve describes the depressive, the malcontent, the anxiety neurotic, and all those who are far more unhappy than they are happy during their normal day-to-day living. Their curve looks like small mounds above the line followed by deep valleys below the line, like this:

Emotional Style No. 2

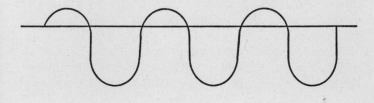

The third pattern describes the withdrawn clients, the ones who insulate themselves from the world by not having intense feelings. They are seldom elated and certainly not depressed. They shield themselves far too effectively to allow for tears or anguish. They are flat in affect and drive normal people around them batty with their coldness and detachment. Guarded personalities are afraid to feel, to be open to possible pain. Such persons are so totally on their guard that they are defending themselves against contact by never allowing themselves highs or lows. Their pattern looks like this:

Emotional Style No. 3

The fourth pattern belongs to the healthy souls who are not afraid of a belly laugh, a good joke, a hug, a kiss, or even tears. They are not afraid to let go and feel pleasure, to dance, to drink or to eat. They like feeling good and aren't the slightest bit guilty over it.

When they notice that they are getting upset, they try to stop this downslide promptly. Unnecessary pain is pointless, so they put their rational knowledge to work as soon as they realize an upset is in the picture. This doesn't mean they have perfect control of their feelings. Instead, it means they are in touch with their feelings to the point where they know when they are beginning to pose a threat. Then they proceed at once to monitor their feelings to prevent them from getting out of hand.

Rational persons can appear serious, sad, concerned, miffed, troubled, can yell at the kids, swear, and shed tears. Normally, however, they do not feel much guilt, inferiority, or self-pity. They are not violent unless in self-defense. Panic and anxiety attacks, fear of disapproval to the point where they permit themselves to be dominated are not typical of these persons. Though they may drink too much at times, they do not make a habit of it. They can overeat on special occasions but watch their diet most of the time. They can goof off at work but make up for it so that they are usually productive. Their curve looks like this:

Emotional Style No. 4

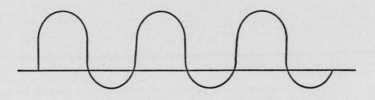

You can see by this curve that rational persons are often irrational—in fact, perhaps as often as disturbed persons are. However, they are to be distinguished from the neurotic by the degree of their pain. It is seldom intense. When the former do act neurotically, it is hoped they apply the principles of RET and pull themselves out of their decline.

The goal of brief therapy is not the complete revamping of the personality but only of those facets which at that time of the client's life are likely to bring his or her feelings a considerable degree below the neutral line.

THREE CRITICAL INSIGHTS

The essence of cognitive restructuring rests in three insights (Ellis, 1962):

INSIGHT NO. 1: Emotional disturbances are caused by our irrational thoughts.

INSIGHT NO. 2: Talking ourselves out of believing those irrational ideas reduces or removes those disturbances.

INSIGHT NO. 3: Nothing else is required.

Insight No. 1 is by now fully appreciated by most serious students of therapy and needs no further defense from me.

Insight No. 2 is also appreciated by all RET therapists at least, even if not by other therapists. However, it is the client most of all who fails to grasp the importance of this insight.

Almost without exception it is the failure to realize the significance of challenging the irrational ideas that causes clients their greatest difficulty. Understanding that an idea is irrational is not all that difficult. Most people agree with you when you confront them relentlessly with irrefutable logic. But that's when they're in your office. Out in the cruel, cold world, at the moment of frustration, old habits take over and the careless client again forgets the rational arguments. For a short while the belief returns that one must be perfect to be worthwhile, or that there are bad people in the world who deserve to be severely punished, or that being rejected is a shattering experience for an adult and must cause great emotional pain.

For example, the man you are counseling wonders what is wrong. Why did he slip? Why, after making fine progress in therapy, did he regress and act as disturbed lately as he had before therapy? The answer is simple, and it is usually the same: he ignored Insight No. 2: emotional disturbances are relieved by *challenging the irrational ideas causing them* (Beck, 1967; Ellis, 1962; Maultsby, 1975).

As the counselor you will focus on why the client failed to do his homework and will get him back on track to debate his self-talk until he feels better. More importantly, you will want to impress on the client the insight that his failure to do this had led to his troubles. Client after client finds this task vexing, or exhausting, and is prone to avoid it. Some clients give up and would rather suffer than work. Some need reminding of how they are forgetting what they learned. And some decide that debating the irrational ideas is not all that important.

At this point the client may insist that the problem must be alleviated, and thus works on the frustration first rather than on the disturbance over it. This could be a sound procedure if the problem is easily and quickly solved. But if it takes time and great effort, it is often better to work on *both* the frustration *and* the disturbance, thereby at least assuring the client some relief before the problem is removed.

Those persons who successfully get relief by working on their problems rather than their emotions may do it the hard way, but they do it regardless. That is sufficiently satisfying to them that they rely on problem-solving from then on and ignore the emotional suffering that might have been avoided had they had Insight No. 2.

Medication and hospital admissions are two other methods people use to avoid the work with Insight No. 2. How much easier they think it is to pop a pill under stress than to face an audience that they're scared of. How much quicker it is to escape unpleasant reality by signing into an inpatient unit of a psychiatric unit (which sometimes resembles a vacation resort) than it is to face their job. These facilities, as necessary as they are, and drugs, as valuable as they are, can easily be misused by people who want to avert the hard work it takes to remain stable and who seek quick relief through the sole efforts of others. Stability and maturity don't come in a bottle. They come from hard work, risk-taking, and the toleration of tension for long periods of time.

Insight No. 3: nothing else but cognitive restructuring is required—not medicine alone, not hospitalization alone, nor the solving of problems alone. The latter, if accomplished, doesn't protect the sufferer against future similar distresses— only the current one.

What about faith? Aren't those who are faithful to a religious creed perfectly capable of withstanding stress without disputing their irrational ideas? It must be stressed that, whether they remain strong despite "neurotic" reasons, as Ellis insists (1962), or because they are watched over by God, the faithful are often able to derive such comfort from their beliefs that the possession of irrational ideas can sometimes be discounted.

ADVISING VS. REASONING

Past therapies made much over the supposed dangers of helping clients too much. That is why advice was shunned in psychoanalysis and nondirective counseling. Today the controversy is still alive and presents the therapist of brief therapy with important questions of priority.

Do you, as a therapist, give advice in brief therapy because it brings quick relief without addressing the irrational ideas? Or is true and valid therapy present *only* when the philosophical foundations underlying the mental distress are dealt with?

Brief therapy takes a clear direction in this matter. Quick relief of pain is our goal. Whether that goal is accomplished through hypnosis, persuasion, advice, prayer, or classical RET therapy makes little difference.

This focus on frustration becomes a legitimate goal. And for good reason. Many clients are simply unwise in the matter of social relationships. Teaching them outright to be smarter with people helps them to be more effective in everyday living and often more rational at the same time.

A young man was ready to quit his job because he was in conflict with the boss. He wanted to leave right away but was upset and sought me out. I had the option of *(a)* teaching him how to keep cool and keep his job or *(b)* giving him some sound advice about not leaving his job until he found another one and then *later* showing him how to get along with difficult authority figures.

If I dealt with the emotional problem first and let him quit before he had another job, I would have taught him something about his anger and how to avoid such conflicts in the future. However, if he quit his job while I was counseling him over his anger, he might have been unemployed for months.

This could indirectly cause him to develop depression and fear, two additional emotional problems.

Giving advice is one of the most important functions a brief therapist performs. It is hoped that the therapist is a mature person, experienced in life, a judge of sane and fair behavior, and intolerant of punitive nonsense. Such a person possesses wisdom about life which would be a waste not to impart when appropriate. Why not save a client a thousand hurts with a few words of good advice? Haven't we all benefited from the hard-earned lessons of our guardians? Why can't we do the same for those who look to us for help? Because they'll become dependent and weak from leaning on us? It's possible, of course. But how many of us were weakened for even a short while by the advice of others? In fact, didn't we benefit by it? Didn't we learn to avoid serious errors? And didn't much of that good advice help us in the whole course of our lives?

Clients coming to me who have been to other therapists have one complaint to make more than any other about their former therapists: "He never told me anything. I just talked and he just listened."

It is apparent to me that clients want information. They want to know what you would do if you were in their shoes. And they have a right to know. If you are going to be a professional counselor, then why hesitate to give counsel? Why must clients be hurt by making errors you can predict? As it is, they don't take our advice enough. I wish they would do it more. When they do, I'm pleased. There are some issues I feel so right about that I don't mind being the authority. And why not? Am I supposed to be in this business twenty-five years and not have something worthwhile to say about life? If you or I can't give sensible information and advice, who can?

THE *R* IN RET

The *R* in RET refers to rational, not reason or rationalization. It is an important distinction to bear in mind.

Rationalizing is a neurotic defense used to avoid uncomfortable or painful truth. That is not what the *R* is all about, obviously.

Reason, on the other hand, covers a broad function under which both rational and irrational fall. You can reason in a rational way or you can reason in an irrational way. The fellow who is calm in a crisis is using reason just as the fellow who is upset during a crisis is using reason. One reasons well (is rational), the other reasons poorly (is irrational).

The neurotic young man cannot be accused of not thinking or of not using his reason. The fault we *can* find with him is that he is not using his intelligence which, if he did use it, would allow him to reason rationally.

He *is* thinking, he *is* reasoning, even when he is in a rage or vomiting from fear. But his thinking and reasoning are incorrect, mistaken, inaccurate, and just plain wrong. When you say 2 plus 2 equals 5, you are wrong of course. But that's not because you didn't think or reason out the answer. You gave the matter your intense thought. You didn't get the answer by breathing deeply, for instance, or by scratching your head. You got it by *using* your head, your brains. The fact that you used your reasoning carelessly is incidental, it is still reasoning, still thinking.

The disturbed young man, therefore, is certainly not a dope who never thinks for himself. He's often a very bright thinker. His problem is that he had one or more poor teachers of psychology as he was growing up. His mother may have taught him to believe that he should think poorly of himself unless he behaved faultlessly. That's rubbish of course, but the young boy couldn't know that. He accepted her teachings and became the same poor reasoner she was. She thought sloppily and she taught her children to think sloppily.

Ironically, the better a student he is, the better he soaks up the neurotic junk his irrational tutors (family, friends, and teachers) pump into him. The best neurotics are simply those who have best absorbed the damaging teachings in childhood. The difference between the healthy and unhealthy personality is, *in part,* the instruction each has received during the formative years, not whether one was weak or strong, bright or dull. These are contributory causes, to be sure, but too often we have overlooked the soundness of the reasoning from the teachers during those formative years.

There is an optimistic message behind this depressive note: a misguided client who comes for therapy can be reassured that help is at hand. For, if one could *passively* learn (and learn extremely well) all sorts of nonsense from misguided instructors, why can't one *actively* learn rational thinking just as well from an expert instructor?

THE *E* IN RET

The appeal to pure reason is often an impotent effort. Although it reflects a fault in the human mentality, it is nevertheless true that most people don't buy cars because of a low index of air resistance. Homes are not purchased because the fuel consumption is 3½ percent less in one than in another. Even silk stockings sell better if pleasantly scented.

The emotive element appears to be a vital ingredient in getting people to change their minds. How can this be accomplished in therapy? By the *way* an idea is expressed in addition to *what* the idea is. To tell a woman client that life is unfair, that she is foolish to pity herself over this unfairness, and that her depression will lift when she accepts that reality is technically correct but often not effective. Such a point, if made in a purely logical and rational manner, would sound like a robot monotonously repeating a recording. Men and women simply do not respond to reason alone, and often less to reason than to feeling.

The psychiatrist has medications, the institutional worker has several occupational and recreational programs, and the psychologist has tests and conversations. In brief counseling, however, the therapist's art of conversing is the best tool to achieve change. While being correct in what one says guarantees some penetration into the thinking of the misguided client, *how* one makes those statements guarantees much greater success. This is where the *E* comes in.

The client who is seriously downcast because the expected

promotion did not materialize need not be barraged with a
string of logical arguments as to why he or she is acting
neurotically. Showing feeling, empathy, and concern are
much more likely to get the despondent person to listen and
feel accepted. Later, when rapport has been established during that session or during the second or third session, an
appeal can be made to his or her irrational ideas. Actually,
in brief therapy, the development of empathy for two or three
sessions at the cost of making rational arguments is not dis-
couraged. Instead, it is important in every session to develop
rapport to the extent that it opens up channels of communication after which important rational messages can be expressed.

You can tell the client that you are sorry to hear of the
bad luck, that you understand the distress caused by failure
to be promoted. Why not make such statements of concern
and understanding? They show compassion and an appreciation of the client's plight. This may be all the client wants
from the counselor. To move too quickly to bring relief does
not allow the client to deal with pain or to express sorrow and
hurt, or to ventilate grievances. Later, when these sentiments
have had an airing, when that vital emotive element has been
recognized, it is appropriate to confront the irrational elements in the case. In the past this process of ventilation was
thought to be a time-consuming one. Sometimes it is. However, we are coming to recognize that if only some part of
each session allows for the expression of feelings, this usually
gives us enough time to do some cognitive restructuring, even
if only during a typical thirty-minute session.

Humor and exaggeration are other powerful emotive factors that not only increase rapport but hasten rational persuasion. The man who insists that he can never forgive himself for a past misdeed can sometimes be reached effectively
if you agree to his unflattering self-appraisals and carry them
a step farther.

He insists he's a rat because of a misdeed and deserves to
be criticized. This time you agree and jokingly insist that he's
got to be the biggest sinner in three counties, that no one is

going to talk to a blackguard like him, and that he might just as well pack his things and take off for the desert, where he can find a cave and become a hermit.

If he insists that he must punish himself in some neurotic way, you can again agree and even stretch the point. "You've got me convinced. I'm beginning to believe that rejection isn't good enough for a cad like you. Tarring and feathering would be fairer. After all, when you're no good at all like you are, what's society to do? Right?"

Each therapist can be facetious according to his own style. Humor supplies a warm, human touch which would clearly be missing if the conversation remained at a cold, rational, and logical level.

In addition to the first two emotive elements—empathy and humor—there is a third: profanity.

Used judiciously, this can be a powerful tool in establishing rapport and opening the ears of *some* clients. The rebellious young man who is in your office because the courts sent him there can be reached more quickly if you use his language at the outset than by all the reasoning in the world. Once he sees he's not talking to a moralizing pedantic, he will often relax and communicate. Though you may regret this observation, you may still find that it establishes rapport quickly.

Once rapport is established, you can continue in that vein or clean up your language as you wish. Many people feel offended by the use of profanity. The poor effect it may have on further sessions or with other prospective clients may indicate that the temporary benefits from using it are far outweighed by the greater losses to your professional well-being.

Nevertheless, the point can still legitimately be made: Profanity, if carefully employed, can help make therapy briefer in two situations. The first is its use with that special population which feels comfortable with such language, and the second is its use to add emphasis to the rational message.

You as a RET therapist have only your verbal skills to perform your work. If you are a rational robot, you will put your client to sleep. To shake up the attention of the inattentive client, a choice expletive or two may be effective. As long as you don't show total stupidity in how you use it, you're likely to benefit on a short-range basis. Don't use profanity with children, dignified elderly ladies, and people whom you suspect find it vulgar. *Respect their sensitivities.* They have every right to be treated with the dignity they expect from professionals.

INTELLECTUALIZING IN RET

The charge is sometimes made that RET with its heavy reliance on the rational process is nothing less than the same old intellectualizing defense with which we therapists are all too familiar. There are clients who can talk a good line and protect themselves from dealing with feelings or from actually doing anything in the real world about their problems.

An excellent example comes to mind. Rubin is a young man in his early twenties. His family history is one of much arguing and little comfort. As a result he became a shy boy, missed out on learning social skills, and was very lonely as an unrequited lover.

I tried in session after session to get him to face his fears and talk to men and women. The more he did this, the sooner he would overcome his social awkwardness and find the happy companionship he was always seeking.

He was naturally threatened by this assignment. To avoid dealing with it, he insisted repeatedly that he had to understand first this and then that aspect of his personality or background before he was ready to do his homework. Try as I might, he intellectualized furiously for months. We debated the most minute issues with the intensity of medieval scholars. After not encountering this defense for at least three months, he came in with a bagful of books (that's right, a bagful) and began grilling me.

It was his belief that he was still dependent on his mother because it was she who taught him to fear rejection. Therefore, ipso facto, if he accepted her thinking still, he must perforce be dependent on her.

I didn't see it that way, but I wasn't interested in debating the issue. It could, in a technical sense, indicate dependency on his mother, but not in the practical sense, since he actually leaned on her very little.

I made the interpretation for the umpteenth time that he wasn't telling me about whom he had met, how many calls he had made, or with whom he ate lunch. His response was to pull out a book on psychology, turn to a page he had previously marked, and read me a passage which I was to explain. Then he wanted me to answer questions about this or that theoretical point. I must say he was mighty provoking at times and I almost lost my rational cool trying to cope with his massive avoidance tactics. But he was bright and challenged me a number of times into deeper thinking about my own beliefs. It always seemed to me that I benefited more by those intellectual exercises than he.

To think in a rational way is not in and of itself intellectualizing. It becomes intellectualizing only when it is used to avoid growth and understanding, when it becomes a smoke screen, so to say. But to reason, to search out knowledge and truth, that's healthy. It requires intelligence, but it is not intellectualizing. What I was trying to get Rubin to do was to *reason,* to use his *intelligence,* so he could learn how he was talking himself into being afraid of rejection. I was trying to break through his habit of intellectualizing, a habit of prostituting his reason and intelligence to *avoid* understanding and growth.

TESTS OF RATIONALITY

Counselors who undertake to use the RET method may never ask: "What makes Ellis and Hauck so right when they claim that there are twelve irrational ideas held by millions of people? Isn't that being arbitrary? Who set these two up as final judges over an idea's rationality or irrationality? God?"

Hardly. Ellis made statements that pass the tests of rationality for his eleven ideas and I hope I did the same for my one. Anyone who examines those ideas can make the determination that these twelve ideas which RET therapists claim are irrational are in fact irrational. They always pass the tests of rationality when examined carefully. As an RET therapist you need to understand when an idea is rational or irrational or you will not have the slightest reason to have any confidence in this method whatever.

An idea is rational if:

1. It conforms to reality.
2. It diminishes self-defeating behavior.

For example, if a male student, insists that he is being rational when he avoids homework because he enjoys television and that this practice, followed routinely, will give him a happy and fulfilled life, we can say with great certainty that he is wrong. He does not pass the tests of rationality because it is simply not true, for instance, that by pleasing himself endlessly on television cartoons or game shows he will adequately prepare himself for this competitive society. Those who have done their homework, become educated, and obtained their degrees usually get better-paying and more attractive positions.

Secondly, by avoiding the hard task of studying, he increases his self-defeating life-style, not diminishes it. The more he goofs off, the more he'll pay in emotional or physical stress someday.

These two tests of rationality can be applied to each of the twelve irrational ideas, and it will be seen upon even cursory examination that they are in fact irrational. The RET therapist had better be acquainted with these two criteria and convinced completely of being correct when this or that thought is termed irrational. The counselor will be challenged on these issues time and time again. Unless the therapist understands why an idea is rational or irrational, there will be little success in convincing anyone else.

RATIONALITY ISN'T EVERYTHING

Those of us who have discovered the peace of mind concomitant with the possession of the principles of rational thinking know only too well how invulnerable we often are to the numerous irritations that so easily bother our brothers and sisters. We daily meet life anew, ready to test each new frustration against our lance of reason, and swagger over the day's battleground, while more sensitive persons are overcome by trials of the moment.

It would seem to me to be a natural consequence for an individual who has mastered the idea that one is not directly responsible for the neurotic reactions of others to be a bit more uncaring about them. A man may reason correctly that his wife's anger is her problem and perhaps flippantly tells her so, again on the ground that nothing he can do short of physical harm can cause her distress. Or he may refuse to observe those little social sensibilities which mean so much to others and behave smugly and tactlessly because he sees no value in observing them. When most persons would lie to the hostess rather than honestly tell her the party was bad, or refrain from obscene language out of deference to her rearing, the thoroughly trained RET person quite often tends toward the opposite.

Because we are only too human, this type of behavior is not rare, for the RET person not only reasons but also rationalizes. A strong tendency of the RET person is to behave self-centeredly, unmindful of the neurotic reactions others may have to this "undisturbing" behavior.

Rightly, of course, it is incumbent upon the neurotic to learn how not to be troubled by the willful behavior, or strong language and ideas, of others. But I quarrel with those persons who use RET in situations where they have little or nothing to lose by not using it. Rational-emotive psychotherapy is, after all, a tool to help oneself remain calm, it is not an instrument to provoke others. When it accomplishes the latter for unnecessary reasons, it is misdirected and abusive. The personality that results from this distortion is hardly a credit to the goal of lowering tension among people.

Such a personality weathers the stares and disapproval of associates with detachment at once admirable in its efficiency, yet icy cold in its indifference. Though much is made in our writings that RET does not create unfeeling robots, let us at least be aware that such a condition is a distinct possibility. Reason can come to our aid when we wish to be calmed and desert us after we have become so.

If rational-emotive therapy is to make truly great contributions to human welfare, it will not suffice merely to make persons undisturbed. It had better also make them civilized. We need not be content to give our clients an inner shield which can deflect the stones hurled at them by a hostile world and then encourage them to throw rocks back.

A person can be content to use RET as a system for self-protection only. Valuing compassion, a person can be sensitive to the potential reactions of others, and when suspecting that an off-color joke would indirectly create embarrassment, desist out of deference to the pain the listeners would bear.

Only when one's own deep values would be violated does the civilized person subject acquaintances to emotionally provoking behavior. In all other instances one can be considerate, kind, warm, and gentle to the fullest of one's abilities. Seen in this light, emotional control does not become an end in itself, but rather a means to an end: the condition of gentility.

This behavior is sometimes lacking among the RET population—be it ever so undisturbed. They often display a bluntness in social intercourse that verges on rudeness. People can do better than merely remain calm.

(The above section, "Rationality Isn't Everything," is adapted from *Rational Living,* Vol. 3, No. 1 (1968), pp. 29–30.)

Chapter 2

The Intake Interview

The intake interview is perhaps the most important session you will have with a client. Sometimes you have only one opportunity to do your thing and if you spoil it, you don't get another chance. If the client respects you even though you're "a shrink," you will have won the client's attention and cooperation. Muff the first interview and you'll never see that client again.

However, aside from the critical issue of gaining respect, the first session enables you to get an idea of the client's problem. In 90 percent of the cases that you'll encounter, comfortable comprehension of the problem will emerge during the first session. A few cases will not require more than one session. Some problems are so circumscribed and some clients are so capable of understanding RET that it takes them only one session to learn what they're looking for. That's great for them, and for you.

THE HALF-HOUR SESSION

For years I have been conducting initial and follow-up sessions that last no more nor less than thirty minutes. In a busy practice there is little alternative. But even if there were, there is simply no need in many instances to conduct longer sessions. After the introductions are over I find I am able to get the vital statistics in about two or three minutes. I try to get a picture of the problem in the next ten to fifteen minutes, counsel for ten or more minutes, and wind up in the last minute or two. In some sessions the dynamics are so obvious that instruction can take place five minutes after the meeting starts. That gives a solid twenty-three minutes to teach RET with two leisurely minutes to wind up setting another appointment and giving a homework assignment.

Once you get into this habit you can go all day. I often see fourteen to sixteen persons a day, a different client almost every half hour. This can be wearing but probably no more so than seeing clients hourly. It has the advantage of giving you a frequent change of pace. Your interest can remain high because the variety of problems is intrinsically stimulating.

But what of the clients? Can they truly get enough help in so short a period? I can assure you the time is perfectly sufficient with the vast majority of clients. There are times, I agree, when you wish you had a double session to work with and sometimes the client too would like more time. For those persons, future sessions can be scheduled for an hour.

For one thing, half-hour sessions cost the client half as much as hourly sessions. That's a solid inducement to persons who do not have insurance coverage. And if you also get over the notion that clients must be seen once a week, you will make counseling even more comfortable for them financially. Many clients welcome the relief of getting good therapy at a fraction of what they anticipated. It has been my practice recently to schedule a client every three or four weeks instead of every one or two weeks as I had been doing for years. My increased case load forced me to spread them out in this manner. I wasn't sure what the effect would be but I was pleasantly surprised. In the majority of the cases the change made no difference whatever. A few, as usual, wanted more frequent visits, but most were (and still are) quite comfortable with a half-hour session every three or four weeks. Frankly I don't prefer that much time between visits, because in the long run those getting fewer sessions improve more slowly. The observation is worth noting, nevertheless, that not all *that* much happens when sessions are not made on a weekly basis.

Half-hour sessions make further sense because longer sessions often mean only a repetition of the material delivered during the first half hour. If you want to concentrate on a circumscribed issue, then it doesn't take forever to explain how a person gets upset. With some experience you can detect the problem, interpret it to the client, whom you can tell for fifteen straight minutes: *(a)* what is causing the upset and *(b)* what the client had better do in the future to avoid those disturbing feelings again. Why bore the poor client by going through the same material in the following twenty minutes?

"What? Allow no time for ventilation; for exploration of causative factors; for the expression of transference feelings?" Not exactly. True, a half hour doesn't allow for these usually lengthy procedures. RET therapists don't avoid them if they stand in the way of movement. If an impasse or a resistance is preventing progress, RET therapists take time with these therapeutic roadblocks just as other therapists do. The big difference between the RET therapists and their long-listening colleagues is that they don't look for these issues. If the issues arise, RET therapists deal with them. But if they can be avoided and progress can still be made, RET therapists will do so. When they have to be dealt with, little time is spent on them. Every so often (in about 5 percent to 10 percent of the cases) brief therapy is an injustice to the complexities of the dynamics encountered. Long-term therapy with all its need for leisure, insight, and exploration into the past may well be the therapy of choice.

One client, Mr. Walls, heard several of my tapes and decided he wanted counseling from me even though he had already been to three therapists. He called long-distance from Chicago, set up an appointment with my secretary, and the following week we talked over the phone for his half-hour session.

After the split-up of his marriage his wife showed a degree of bitterness he didn't expect. She made any interaction be-

tween them as annoying as possible. To be on the receiving
end of so much hatred made him feel alienated.

But that wasn't all. She managed to brainwash his children so completely against him that they didn't want to visit
him, speak to him over the phone, or answer his letters. They
never thanked him for his presents and they did not reciprocate on his birthday, even with a token gift or a card.

Nor was that all. His mother turned against him too.
When he called her on Mother's Day she hung up. Talk
about rejection—this fellow could write a book!

He was hurt and angry. And I couldn't blame him. However, feeling sorry for him would not help, so I decided to
show him how he could live more calmly with the situation.
In the remainder of the half hour I described his depression
as resulting from self-pity from being so massively rejected.
I pointed out that he had better regard all those people as
unforgiving neurotics who were best left alone. Then I helped
him see that they had a right to their unfair and impolite
ways and just because he didn't approve of such behavior
didn't mean they had to change. Then I questioned him
throughly to ascertain the degree of comprehension he had
obtained from my long explanations. He asked a couple of
questions and seemed to understand my views quite well.

I wound up the session with a request that we set up
another appointment to explore why and how he managed to
get all his loved ones turned against him. He would do that
when he knew his schedule better, he said. That's the last I
heard of him for several months.

I had given a speech and a young man introduced himself
to me afterward. It was Mr. Walls. He got word of my talk
through some acquaintances in the area and decided to make
the trip to Rock Island from Chicago to meet me.

He was feeling great, he claimed. I had told him exactly
what he needed to know to deal with the cruel and selfish
behavior of his family. Though he was still trying stubbornly
to make friends with his mother and children, just as stubbornly they were still rejecting him.

He had thought over my invitation to explore their hostility but decided he knew what caused it and that it had no direct relationship to him. He had made a mistake to marry a clever paranoid who could charm less critical thinkers to her side, and that analysis satisfied him. In the meanwhile he was going with a nice woman and his life was looking up again.

I hope his improvement has not wavered. It would surprise me if it has. Take note, he did little ventilation, we didn't get into any historical material that could explain the development of the problem. We simply focused on the here and now, on the unpleasant way he was being treated, on his reactions and what *he* could do about *his reactions.* It was clear that not much was going to be done about the family itself. Even later, that problem remained unchanged. Yet he felt better because his thinking about the problem had changed: another piece of evidence to support the ABC theory of emotions.

GET ONLY AS MUCH BACKGROUND INFORMATION AS YOU NEED TO UNDERSTAND THE FRUSTRATION

A young executive came to me recently with complaints of free-floating anxiety, fears of death, and fears of cancer. I learned only that he came from a strict religious background, that the symptoms were increasing as his work demands increased, but that he could offer no other reason why he would develop the symptom since he entered the executive ranks.

I then proceeded to educate him about anxiety itself and hoped that simply teaching him how he makes himself nervous would be enough to bring him relief and might at the same time get him to tell me what he was saying to himself that could bring on these anxiety states.

There was only mild improvement from this technique. I realized then I would have to go into deeper history to help find out what he was thinking of before he became tense. During this probing I learned that he was practically totally untroubled when he was away from the office and on vacations. Taking this as my clue, I thought I would probe more deeply into his work habits and his history of drive and achievement. It was then that I learned that he had achieved statewide recognition as a track star while in high school and that he was now in a business which took him out of the office several mornings a week to seven o'clock meetings, kept him at the office until six or six thirty, and brought him back to the office after dinner until late at night. Once I understood the great demands he was placing on himself (which I was only able to learn through a more extensive history-taking) I was able to focus on the true source of the problem: his belief that he has to be outstanding in all possible respects. This justified his long hours and his excessive drive over a period of years.

This is all the history-taking that was necessary to bring the relief he wanted. It was not necessary to delve into his parental relationships, his sex life, and many other areas, because they were not relevant toward understanding the frustration. Once that was achieved, the primary work of understanding his difficulty was over.

It is hoped that the days of psychoanalytic inquiry are past. We can begin to be somewhat selective about what we need to know about people. I think the above example clearly demonstrates that it is not necessary for us to go into the deep history of a person, if the data relevant to the issue are more readily at hand. I think "relevancy" is the key word in helping the counselor understand what is wise to look into and what is superfluous to look into.

The novice counselor will require experience to know how to focus on relevant issues quickly. Until this skill is developed, it is perhaps wiser to take more history than is necessary rather than less. In time a technique for cutting through irrelevancies with ease will be perfected. For the present, however, go slowly and cautiously.

DON'T BE STARTLED BY
THE PRESENTING COMPLAINT

A great way to lose the confidence of your client is express shock or mirth if his symptom is a bit unusual. One client dreaded coming to me for counseling because he thought I'd laugh when he told me his symptom. He had an obsessive thought that he had to shower if he had an erotic thought of his girl friend. I later met her and discovered she was a real beauty. I then began to realize that he practically lived in the shower.

I did not laugh at his symptom and so we got along just fine. I have long since learned to be prepared for almost anything clients say. Some will tell you they are gay, others that they want to bury a hammer in a child's head. In one case, a young man couldn't go out of a store unless he left by the very same route he entered. This really presented problems in a supermarket that always directs traffic in one way and out another. If you allow yourself to have sport at a client's expense, you do it at the cost of lengthening therapy. It strains trust and this will have to be repaired before movement is likely to occur.

Be sophisticated and worldly, and unshockable·if you can. A lady came to me one day because she wanted help with her annoying tendency to look at people's feet when she first meets them. She gets the urge to ask people to remove their shoes and socks so she can see their feet. If they are the slightest bit deformed, crooked, or with a single corn, she feels compelled to reject the person. When you can take a symptom like that in stride, you've matured. And if you can't? Do more and more counseling until familiarity breeds nonchalance.

ESTABLISH THE ACTIVATING EVENT
AND THE IRRATIONAL IDEAS

The heart of RET is in knowing what the frustration (Activating Event) appears to be which is indirectly causing the distress and the irrational ideas (iB) the client has over the stressful events.

There appear to be three types of clients with respect to these two conditions:

1. Some clients find it difficult to detect the Activating Event (A).
2. Some clients find it difficult to detect what they are saying about the event (iB).
3. Some clients find it difficult to detect either.

Mae developed blinding headaches at different times and on irregular days. I tried to elicit information that would help me understand what she was telling herself about her problems, but surprisingly she didn't have the vaguest idea of what was troubling her. We explored her marital relationships, her feelings for her children, her neighbors, and her career. All drew a blank.

I find it hard to believe that someone can be upset repeatedly by an event and not know what it is. But it's the truth. It happens all the time. It is the second most frequent of the three problems. The most frequent is not knowing what the irrational beliefs are.

I asked Mae to think hard about the connection between her headaches and certain events in her life. If there was no connection, I would be inclined to believe that her headaches were physically, not psychologically, caused.

In a short while I felt we were on the right track. I used a technique I call playing Sherlock Holmes. In short, I play detective and try to find out under what circumstances the symptom occurs. There is a pattern, a gestalt, a sensible connection between one event and another, all having common elements which help create the symptom.

I asked Mae when she had her last severe headache. She reported having it last Friday night after she and her husband returned from a party.   .

"You had the headache when you arrived home or after

you were home a while?" I asked.

"We had a great time at the party, so I can't think I got it there. No, it must have been after we got home."

"What happened?"

"Nothing. Jim took the baby-sitter home. That was all. I was feeling all right, come to think of it. But it was while he was gone that I began to feel the ache coming on. I remember, because I wanted to ask him where the aspirin was and he wasn't there."

"Why would you have been upset while he was gone?"

"I don't know. Do you think there's a connection? What could it be?"

"You said you felt okay until after he left with the baby-sitter. There might have been something in that event which threatened you," I suggested.

"Such as?"

"What does the baby-sitter look like?"

"Oh, I see what you mean. She's just a nice adolescent. I certainly don't worry about her. But come to think of it, do you suppose I was troubled by Jim's behavior?"

"What do you mean?"

"I noticed he put his arm over her shoulder as he was escorting her to the car and he was gone much longer than I thought was needed to take her home."

Further probing revealed that she had a small feeling of distrust in regard to her husband. We checked this hypothesis with other events that gave her cause to wonder about him and in each case she developed a headache within an hour.

For the RET therapist this is only the beginning. Since it is not A that causes our disturbances, we continue on to B as soon as we understand clearly what A is.

"Mae, does that suggest how you are upsetting yourself?"

"It seems I feel threatened when Jim ignores me or shows attention to others. That's when I get angry. I don't show it, but develop a headache instead."

So far so good. To complete this investigation, Mae had better know what she is *telling* herself when she feels rejected. It is not enough to know she is threatened by the loss of Jim's love. She wants to know *how* she is upsetting herself over that.

Mae suggested, "I'm probably telling myself that Jim finds other women more attractive than me."

"Maybe so, Mae. But that can't cause you to be upset."

"It can't? Why not?"

"Because it could be true."

"Of course it could be true. So?"

"So that thought can't upset you then."

"Why not?"

"Because we find that when people are upset it is because they have told themselves something foolish, silly, stupid, false, or irrational."

"Well, what's so silly about what I said about Jim?"

"That you could be upset by his paying attention to others. That's perfectly possible. Therefore it cannot account for your disturbance."

"So what *is* causing my headaches?"

"Other thoughts. The irrational ones. What else are you telling yourself?"

"He might leave me."

"But, Mae, that's perfectly possible too. Therefore that idea can't cause serious emotional pain."

"What? Are you telling me that losing my husband isn't supposed to hurt?"

"That's right. Of course I'd expect you to be unhappy about losing him, and I'd expect you to be in low spirits for a time until you got your bearings. But I insist you don't *have* to get upset over losing your mate unless you allow it."

"What do you mean by that?"

"By telling yourself irrational things *over* his leaving you."

"Such as?"

"Such as two things: 'It would be the end of the world if Jim ever stopped loving me,' and 'I'm not much of a person if he doesn't find me acceptable.' "

"I don't get it," she responded with a puzzled look on her face.

"Those are the two irrational ideas causing your head-aches. You think they're rational, reasonable, sensible, and true. That is why you're hurt deeply after you have those thoughts. If I can get you not to think that way, you won't get upset."

"You mean even if Jim leaves me someday?"

"Yes."

"That's going to take some doing," she said with a smile.

"I know," was my response.

NOTE: If clients can tell you what they are upset about, it is relatively easy for you to suggest what they might be saying to themselves over the problem. For instance, if you learn from John that someone broke a promise to him you can rest assured he is either making himself angry by believing people *must* be reliable because that is the way he wants people to behave, or he is making himself depressed because he is feeling sorry for himself. These are safe assumptions to make even though you have not talked to him about them. The irrational ideas are usually easy to detect.

But getting a clear idea of A (the Activating Event) is another matter. Until you know what he is upsetting himself over, you can hardly be sure you know what he's telling himself. You can only make general statements about his self-verbalizations, but they would be imprecise and therefore not terribly helpful.

For example, for practically all depressed clients you can automatically assume they are blaming themselves, pitying themselves, or pitying someone else. And for angry clients, you can almost be certain they are blaming someone and insisting that they, the clients, must have their own way.

Though this can be helpful, it is helpful only up to a point. Much more importantly would be knowing *what* the client is feeling pity or anger over. To know that, we must know the events the client is responding to. Then we can get a much clearer idea as to the person's thinking.

Bruno was falling out of love with his wife. He felt guilty over this but couldn't help it. And he couldn't tell me why he didn't love his wife. The usual listening didn't help him put two and two together to make sense of his sudden dislike for his wife.

Again I played Sherlock Holmes and found out that the symptom had started only three years ago. He was happily married for ten years then suddenly developed this symptom. What happened three years ago? Their first child was born. Bingo! Now, in a flash, because I had A, I could easily guess at iB.

I reasoned that Bruno was jealous of the time his child received from his wife and that he told himself *(a)* he must be loved more than the child or it would prove he was second best and *(b) that would be horrible*.

Further inquiry proved this to be completely correct, though getting him to ignore her necessary attentions to her children proved fruitless. He was so hurt over sharing her (due to a childhood problem of not being the favored of three siblings) that he ultimately divorced his wife.

I've found that the precipitating event can often be detected if the counselor will pay close attention to the time factor. Try to reconstruct the past in your mind so you can imagine what the client went through.

For example, if your client develops anxiety over college work, find out *(a)* when the anxiety first appeared and *(b)* what happened about that time which might account for it. Then you can guess at the irrational ideas responsible for the disturbance.

If a young man says he became tense during the first week of the fall semester of his junior year, you would want to know: *(a)* did he have rooming problems such as not finding a suitable roommate, *(b)* was that a new college for him, away from home, without friends, or *(c)* was he under pressure to get top grades because he needed them for graduate school, or to please his folks, or merely to stay in school? Skillful questioning can zero you in quickly in most instances and then you can figure out what he's saying to himself.

PROBING FOR A PROBLEM

In brief therapy the idea is to be brief. Enough of this hemming and hawing. You have limited time at your disposal, so cut through the verbiage and get to the point. Control the session. You have the psychological compass and had better steer a straight and true course from start to finish if you want your client to gain from the encounter with you.

In the following transcribed demonstration session you will get an idea of how active an RET therapist can be. The subject is a volunteer from the audience at a workshop I conducted. Such demonstration interviews usually leave a great deal to be desired because they are not bona fide and spontaneous calls for help. They are performed partially to do the therapist a service. For this reason the volunteer hesitates to speak of areas of his living which are not significant problems. Yet, with a directive approach we soon see that he too has a number of areas that could justify therapeutic attention any time he is so inclined, particularly the problem of blaming himself over his ex-girl friend's feelings.

THERAPIST: What's your problem, Rolland?

CLIENT: I don't really have a problem, I guess. I really don't know what I am supposed to talk about. I guess you could say that I keep to myself too much. I can't relate to people that well. I am sort of quiet. I keep things to myself too much.

T: How bad does that get? Explain that a little bit further.

C: I don't think it's too bad. It is just one of my things, you know. I am not upset with it.

T: But you would like to be a little bit more forward socially, would you? Or a little bit more at ease socially?

C: Not necessarily.

T: Do you like the way you are?

C: Yes, I like the way I am.

T: Okay, let's talk about a problem then.

C: I don't have any big problems. I . . . I am perfectionistic, I guess.

T: Explain that.

C: I like everything to be just right and I know it can't be that way, but I still strive for perfection. A lot of times when I don't get it just how I want it I get a little upset.

T: Okay, how upset do you get?

C: Well, not too upset ... just ... I really don't get that upset at all. That's just the way it is.

T: It is not a problem in other words.

C: That's right. See ... I wish somebody else in here had one.

T: Okay, let me fish for something then. Do you ever get angry?

C: Yes, I suppose.

T: See? We've got something going already. We can start pursuing that one. Do you ever get depressed?

C: Yes.

T: Okay, we could start pursuing that. Do you ever get nervous or afraid?

C: Not as much as I get depressed.

T: Do you ever worry?

C: Yes.

T: Okay, you see we've got three cardinal neurotic problems we could talk about. Do you ever show lack of good self-discipline?

C: Oh, sure!

T: We've got four good problems. Now which of these problems do you think you are most bothered by: depression, anger, nervousness and worry, or poor self-discipline? Which of those would be the most bothersome problem to you?

C: All about the same I guess.

T: Well, pick one.

C: Depression.

(Note how methodically and quickly a problem has been targeted. Much of this fishing was resistance before an audience and it is quite understandable. The same often happens in one-to-one therapy, however. When it does, be advised to move things along until an agreement has been reached that an issue exists which is worth pursuing.)

T: Okay, what are you depressed about? When do you get depressed?

C: When I am not doing things as well as I could.

T: Such as?

C: Oh, I am not as . . . oh . . .

T: Give me an example of the last time you got depressed even though it was not serious but you were depressed somewhat.

C: Okay. Last week I was depressed about my situation with my ex-girl friend. You know, I wish I could have handled the situation better.

T: You handled something badly with respect to her?

C: Right.

T: Do you understand how you became depressed?

C: I just felt that I hurt somebody unnecessarily . . . sort of . . .

T: How?

C: I was too blasé, you know. I just kind of . . . I don't know. I didn't show . . . I wasn't feeling the same things she was feeling. So you know, I felt bad that I didn't . . .

T: Because you hurt her feelings?

C: Yes.

T: You are feeling guilty because of the harm you supposedly caused her. What happened?

C: She found out that I didn't feel the same way about her as she felt about me.

T: That's how you hurt her feelings?

C: Yes.

T: Now can you analyze in some depth how you hurt her feelings?

C: She wanted it to be the same way and found out that it wasn't that way.

T: Okay, that's true. That's what you said before. But I am asking, How can that literally hurt her feelings?

C: I don't know. She was planning one thing and then her plans got sidetracked, I guess.

T: Yes, I understand that. That's what you said before. I am asking, How did that hurt her? You said you hurt her by doing that, by disappointing her. You mean to say that every time a person is disappointed that the person who does the disappointing is responsible for that person's pain?

C: No, no.

T: Well, that's what you're saying.

C: No, not really.

T: What are you saying?

C: I don't really know what I am saying. I don't know.

T: Tell me, did you hit her when you told her this?

C: No.

T: Did you throw her in a cold shower when you were talking to her?

C: No.

T: Give her pneumonia?

C: No, nothing physical.

T: Nothing physical?

C: Well, no. I guess I wouldn't . . . no.

T: It was an emotional hurt that we are talking about?

C: Yes.

T: Okay, you are saying that you hurt your girl friend emotionally.

C: I guess.

T: That's not possible.

C: Okay.

T: Okay? What is okay?

(The debate has started. We are now in the midst of the therapeutic process. He believes his irrational ideas that he can upset someone emotionally and I dispute this. I will pursue this until he acknowledges that I am right, or until I acknowledge that I am wrong and he is right, or until time runs out.)

C: Well, I read about something like that yesterday, how she hurts herself.

T: Right.

C: I know what you are going to say.

T: Well, what am I going to say?

C: She hurts herself by her thoughts.

T: About what she says to herself?

C: Right.

T: About what?

C: The situation.

T: The situation that you presented her with?

C: Right.

T: Okay, are you saying, "I am a rotten guy because I hurt her after she said some silly things to herself in connection with what I did"? Who *is* responsible for her thinking?

C: Well, I guess . . .

T: Well, say it.

C: She is, I guess.

T: Why is it so hard to say?

C: Well, I just feel that . . . I hate to see when people feel bad.

T: Then why didn't you help her overcome feeling bad?

C: Because to do that I would have had to hurt her even worse later probably.

T: What do you mean?

C: Well, the way to help her was to say everything was all right between us.

T: Beautiful. Thank you. I was hoping you would say that. Now isn't there any other way you could have helped her over that problem without necessarily satisfying her frustration?

C: That's what I tried to do, but it didn't work out.

T: What was it you tried?

C: I just explained to her the way things were.

T: And she decided what?

C: That I was causing her to be upset.

T: She refused to believe that you weren't upsetting her?

C: Yes.

T: And how did you react?

C: I knew that I was upsetting her.

T: Wait, I am saying that you are not now and did not then upset her.

C: Oh.

T: You didn't upset her.

C: Yes, you're right.

(Notice how he is being encouraged to challenge his beliefs? He already knows some RET theory from previous study, but here we see him easily slipping back into irrational thinking. In a moment we will see why he is so unsure of himself: he's not convinced.)

T: You didn't upset her but you didn't tell her that either. She still believes that you are a louse because you are responsible for her feelings?

C: Right.

T: She still carries that grudge around against you and holds you responsible for what who did?

C: She did.

T: For what she did! Good! So if you had really wanted to help her, what could you have told her?

C: I didn't think I could tell her anything except what I told her.

T: Why couldn't you have told her what I just told you now? Why didn't you do her a favor by literally telling her how she is getting upset?

C: I didn't tell her that.

T: I know it but wouldn't that have been a real service?

C: Oh, yes, but she probably would have said, "You're crazy!"

T: That's got nothing to do with the point.

C: How's that?

T: The point is that she would have said that you are crazy and she would have held you responsible for upsetting her. Correct?

C: Yes.

T: But that's neither here nor there. That's only because she hasn't learned what you and I have learned. And maybe it's about time you started to teach her. Then you would at least have put her on the road to good mental health by making her responsible for what?

C: Herself.

T: Her own disturbance, yes. She thinks you can remove her frustrations. Well, if you can do that and it doesn't bother you too much to remove the frustration, tell her you love her. If you can be honest about it, say it. But if you don't think you can do that, say: "Listen, I can't lie to you and if you want to get upset about it, I can give you some good advice or I can send you to someone who can give you therapy, or I can give you some good reading. Anyway, you are giving yourself a bad time. You are acting self-defeatingly and you don't have to and I hope you get over your pain very quickly." Now that would have been good therapy.

C: Yes.

T: If you had done that, if you had seen it as I am seeing it here, would it have been possible for you to be depressed?

C: Not if I went along the lines that you're suggesting.

T: Why not?

C: Because it wasn't me. She was the one who brought on her feelings.

T: What would you have had to feel guilty about?

C: Nothing.

T: You would have felt guilty about absolutely nothing. If you are not feeling guilty about something, how can you be depressed?

C: Right.

T: Isn't that beautiful?

C: Yes, that's great. You should have been there.

T: What does she look like? Maybe I'll join you! Seriously, this is the way to handle these kinds of things. You are not responsible for someone else's emotional behavior. You are simply telling her something you have every right in the world to tell her. Which is what?

C: My true feelings.

T: Yes, right. And they are no longer exactly what she wants them to be and that's just too bad.

C: Yes, right.

T: And that's the way it goes. And if she can't take that the minute she loses a relationship, she had better learn. Now is a good time to teach her because that's the way life is.

You never know whom you are going to make music with later. Love is always a gamble. You took the gamble. She took a gamble. It just didn't work out on your end, so you have a right to back out.

(We come now to the end of the session and concluding remarks are in order. He is reminded again of what happened during the interview and how he can avoid future depression from self-blame.

(However, this is the time to get him thinking of what else he could do to help himself and why future sessions might be in order. In this way we encourage a follow-up of this session and a journey into areas he hadn't even thought of.)

T: Now isn't this interesting. You said you had no problems and yet we have been talking about a very common problem for about a half hour about this tendency to blame oneself for other people's behavior. I am sure that if we go into this farther, you will see that there are numbers of times when you have done this kind of thing and blamed yourself.

If we want to get off self-blame entirely, we can explore the other forms of depression. I am sure that you have sometimes pitied yourself or pitied others and have been depressed in those two ways besides just this one.

Or we could talk about anger. I can show you how you make yourself angry, and how you can avoid these things in the future. The same is true of nervousness or worry or fear or poor self-discipline. These are all psychological problems. And it is interesting because you started out saying, "Well, I don't have any problems."

C: I really don't. Those are minor ones.

T: They are minor ones. I am sure you are basically a fairly well adjusted person who every so often does what every normal person does. What?

C: Occasionally acts neurotically.

T: As I do, and all of us do. Every so often that's what we expect as human beings. And the more we reduce these things the better off we are. And that's all.

STEP BY STEP IN THE FIRST SESSION

There is a routine to the first interview. After you observe the sequence in detail, try to make it automatic so you can avoid thinking of it. That's when it works best, when you know it well enough to do it by heart and can also veer away from it without fear of getting lost.

Step 1: Collect routine data.

Get the client's name, age, address, phone number, spouse's name, age, occupation, occupation of the client, who referred the client (so you can write a letter of thanks), and where the client and spouse work.

Step 2: Determine the problem, if possible.

Simply ask, "How may I help you?" or "What seems to be the problem?" or "What can I do for you?"

You can delay such a direct assault for a few moments by commenting on the weather, on a news event, or on the neat suit the man is wearing or the lovely dress the woman is wearing. And after you've said those niceties, get to the point and give your clients their money's worth by trying to learn how they are upsetting themselves, and (for the moment) *what* they are upsetting themselves over. During this phase you'll be listening for problems, real-life problems, the kind most of us get bent out of shape over. Listen for conflicts between husbands and wives, parents and children, employers and employees. Listen for failure of accomplishment, rejection from significant others, or the tendency to blame oneself or others.

Let the client talk. You can't learn these important facts if you dominate the conversation. In brief therapy this process takes anywhere from five to fifteen minutes. By that time you have some idea of what part of the problem is. And you can make recommendations about the problem thus far uncovered. In the remainder of the session you can at least send the client out of your office better educated than before. And after the session the client can go home and mull over your instructions.

Step 3: Ask questions.

In brief therapy you dare not sit back and let the client talk on as though you had all the time in the world. You want to learn what the problem is, but often the client may ramble so much and give you so many problems that you won't be able to get your bearings. To avoid this, you had better take charge and ask questions. Find out who is involved in the problem, when it occurs, under which circumstances, and how the client reacts to the problem. By probing politely you are easily able to get your bearings in fifteen minutes' time.

In rare instances it is important to make an exception. Some persons want to unload and ventilate and nothing more. When you get the feeling that your client doesn't want your advice at all but only wants to complain, you can tell readily enough because the person won't listen to you. So shut up, lean back in your chair, smile, nod your head from time to time, and let your client get those feelings out in the open. This is a free ride. It's a relaxing session, sometimes a boring session. In any event there isn't much you can do about it, so you might just as well enjoy it and relax.

Step 4: Select a problem.

Most people have a number of emotional and situational problems all at the same time. When they enter counseling they have a strong tendency to tell you about first this then that problem and often spiel off a list of complaints that won't quit until you put a stop to them. It's frankly a waste of time to listen to the whole life story when you can deal with only one problem at a time. So interrupt the client's recitation of lamentations. The young man may think you want his life history. Disappoint him gently. Ask him not to go on with all the problems he can think of but instead decide which of his problems is the most distressing and to which he wants you to address yourself. Then get to it straightaway and begin his education.

Step 5: Formulate the dynamics.

After you have selected one target problem, try to get a clear understanding (for yourself for the time being) as to what is going on. You want to be able, if possible, to make a coherent statement about what is causing your client's distress. This personal formulation will usually be incomplete, but don't be timid about arriving at a hypothesis nevertheless. These tentative formulations are like the blueprints a contractor uses in erecting a building, or they are to you what a map is to a navigator. If you have no idea what the problem is, how the client is working himself up into a lather over it, and how this problem probably fits into the usual patterns of his life, you simply won't know if you're being relevant and helpful.

A married woman in her thirties comes to you expressing dissatisfaction over her home life. Husband, children, parents, and in-laws are all draining her with constant expectations of service. She is tearful, confused over whether she has a moral right to protest against the whole clan, and is fearful that she'll be deserted by everyone if she rocks the boat and asserts herself.

Before going into your educational phase to teach her that rejection does not hurt, see if you can understand how long she has been a passive personality. Who held acceptance and rejection over her head as a child? More often than not you'll get the answer in a short sentence: "My mother," "My brother ran my life," "I am adopted and my parents always threatened to give me up if I didn't mind."

Let her explain her passivity briefly to see how it is a thread weaving in and out of the many relationships she is involved in. A pattern may emerge that ties her fearfulness from her parents to her in-laws, to her husband, then to her children, and co-workers and neighbors.

When you can formulate a statement of the case, you will have a fine grasp on the problem and will not likely lose your bearings over the weeks and months that follow. The following is a tentative formulation of the case we have been discussing: "This woman has little confidence in herself and feels she can't survive without the approval of those around her because she thinks she's worthwhile only when she's loved. Being thought well of was literally a realistic concern of hers when she was a child because her parents died and she could never depend on the changing moods of her adoptive parents. To get along she learned to give in. She has kept peace with her husband and children for the very same reasons. Now, after trying desperately for years to gain security by being a giver she feels so wrung out and unhappy she is deeply depressed.

"I want to get her to see the differences between the danger she was in as a child and the danger she is in today. Then I'll teach her to assert herself, first against the most distant relationships, and gradually work up so she can deal with her family. Getting her to question her inferiority and neurotic need to be loved (rather than her sensible desire to be loved) and then getting her to live through several rejections may give her the proof she requires to realize her hidden strengths."

Armed with this mental road map we are ready for the next step.

Step 6: Educate the client.

Now that you've decided which problem you want to work on with this woman, start her education by telling her in plain language how she upsets herself, how she can regain her composure, and if necessary, explain any dynamics you gain insight into. It is during this phase of the first session that you do most of the talking. You educate her purely and simply and even ask questions from time to time to see whether she is following you.

However, don't be a preacher. This is still supposed to be a conversation, so don't make a boring sermon or a paternal lecture out of a pleasant encounter with a human being who wants understanding, not condescension. For no matter how much you may be able to serve your client, she can sometimes enlighten you. Even with all your skill, don't forget your sense of humility.

Step 7: Summary and quiz

When you have introduced the client to a new view of her problem (your formulation), ask her to tell you what you've been saying. This is the feedback you want in order to assess her comprehension of the problem, about the way she has disturbed herself over it, and about what you want her to do until you see her again.

Correct her summary statement of the problem at this point: "No, I didn't say it wasn't important if you were rejected. Of course it's important. You'd be disturbed if you didn't care at all if no one thought well of you. What I said was that it is not the end of the world if someone rejects you. Do you see the distinction? What did I say the reason was for your passivity?"

"You said I was passive because I've always been dominated."

"No. That's not what I said. Being dominated is indirectly part of the reason for your problem today. When you were a child it was natural to expect you to be passive in the company of powerful adults. But now you're an adult and your children are dominating you. How do you explain that?"

"Because I'm afraid they won't like me."

"That's true. You are afraid they won't like you. Since it's true, rational, and sensible, that statement doesn't account for your fear."

"Well, what does?"

"See if you can pick it out. Remember, to make yourself upset you have to say irrational things to yourself. You're making good sense when you suggest that your children will reject you if you displease them."

"You have me stumped. What irrational thing am I saying to myself?"

"That it would be unbearable if your children rejected you. Get it?"

In this manner the finer points of the session can be firmed up and any misunderstanding clarified. But one exercise is

hardly likely to perform wonders. It does provide the therapist with a parting shot at bringing the lesson to a close.

Step 8: Assign homework.

"Seeing is believing." This is the basis for assigning homework to your client. A more accurate way of expressing this
would be, "Experiencing is believing." In some cases, however, it is not necessary to have proof at all that a situation
is harmful or not. Reason itself is sometimes all that is
needed.

Can we survive the rejection of our parents if we are
adults? Of course we can. Why wouldn't we be able to? Even
if we haven't been disowned *yet,* we can surely see that it
would not be a life-and-death issue unless we were bedridden
and absolutely needed the care of our loved ones, and we
lived where no social or charitable services were available.
Barring that condition we'd survive. Logic tells us so.

Logic also tells us that rejection is usually not all *that*
distressful. We don't actually have to experience all degrees
of rejection to know that being turned down at the altar is
a great deal more difficult to handle than being turned down
by the PTA for the position of crossing guard.

Be this as it may, people are often more convinced by
proof than reason alone and it is for this reason that homework assignments are given. They are made precise and
somewhat exaggerated because counselors anticipate the natural tendency of persons to goof off. And they are most
effective for habits involving fear. People seem to require
proof that this or that is not harmful. By counselors urging
them to face their fears people learn how painful (or painless)
the fears really are.

Rejection is probably the greatest fear most people have
and this causes shyness, social isolation, and lack of assertiveness. Assigning the male client the task of calling up old
friends to attend the movies will help him experience the
actual degree of pain. He can repeatedly compare his anticipated pain with actual pain. Asking him to enter a candy
store and ask the clerk for a pound of hamburger, and stutter

all the while helps him fight his tendency to feel shame and embarrassment. The fellow who is afraid of women is assigned the task of talking to several ladies each day. If he talks to only one every other day, he may learn with complete conviction that he has appeal for *some* females. This is one of those problems he would not likely have been able to work through with logic alone. He could have, of course, if he had merely observed human behavior. Practically every ugly duckling has a mate and some of the most stunning females marry sloppy and ugly men. Logically, therefore, he would have been completely rational to believe his time will come if he searches long enough. He *could* have done that but most people won't. They need the proof to be convinced.

Therefore, do not spend session after session trying to convince with disputation what a single experience may achieve. The client may welcome the former because it is safe and harmless. Do not let this happen. Bring the world and all its reality into your office with you. Don't discuss a problem in a vacuum. Unless all the fine theory of therapy is eventually translated into changed behavior, nothing much has been accomplished. For most people the proof of the pudding is in the eating.

For the shy, prescribe dancing lessons, phone calls to people they have always wanted to meet, or brazenly sitting at the lunch table of the group that is feared. Have them do shame-combating exercises such as wearing a silly T-shirt, asking strangers for the whereabouts of city hall right in front of that building, or paying bus fare with pennies slowly counted out to the driver, with a deliberate stutter all the while.

For the unassertive, suggest that they ask for their loans to be repaid, to say, "No" to family members when they want to borrow the car or to fix something for them at an inconvenient time. When the boss asks on the spur of the moment that they work overtime, advise them to refuse *just for the practice* (assuming your clients would not lose their jobs to do so).

In the same way assignments can be dreamed up to combat guilt, self-pity, other-pity, anger, and procrastination. The counselor will want to give this some thought and develop a repertoire of homework activities for each problem.

Along with the homework, however, it is important to get the clients to reward or penalize themselves in accordance with how well they have performed their homework. If they have followed instructions faithfully each day, they might reward themselves with a special dessert, a movie, or a small gift. If they do well over a week's or a month's period, the reward can be correspondingly more impressive. Perhaps they can now allow thesmselves a ski trip, a new suit, a trade-up in a car.

However, if they fail to fulfill their homework assignments, they are to penalize themselves in such a way that they cannot get out of the arrangement. Should they fail to lose the weight or to give up smoking, or to complete painting the house, they can agree to give away a prized possession, or to do something particularly distasteful or boring. For example, they might volunteer to wash their neighbor's car or kitchen floor. And if they really want to put pressure on themselves, they could use an old RET penalty that goes like this: give your friend money to hold to be donated to the political party you despise the most if you do not meet your goals. Along with that you will have written a letter to the donatee telling how you have admired his or her work for years, how you want to support his or her efforts, and that the funds can be used in any way. Can you imagine the motivation this can build if the donor is black and the other party is the Klu Klux Klan, or if the donor is a liberal and the friend would donate to the Republican Party?

Homework assignments also include taking psychological tests (if you feel they can help) and recommended reading. Not everyone enjoys reading or gets much from reading. I therefore ask clients before recommending bibliotherapy if they like to read. If they don't, I pass over the reading assignments. If they enjoy books and get a lot from them, I do not hesitate to refer them to any book I feel is helpful.

The Institute for Rational Living in New York City has an extensive booklist of RET writings which I often use. I prefer to refer my clients to books which are relatively inexpensive, which focus on a single emotional complex such as depression, anger, etc., and which deal with complex psychological ideas in nontechnical language. I hope I have achieved these ends in my own writings (see References).

Step 9: Schedule future appointments.

Should you decide by now that additional counseling is needed, you will want to point this out a minute or so before the session is over.

You can get into the subject quite directly by merely saying: "I'll have to see you again. Please make an appointment with my secretary that is at your convenience."

Or you can explain your reasons for wanting future sessions. "Teaching you two how to get along with each other is going to take time. I'd be prepared for about a half dozen sessions, one every two to four weeks. Is that all right with you?"

A TYPICAL INITIAL INTERVIEW

The following transcript has been altered in minor ways to protect the identity of the client. (All counseling transcripts in this book have been similarly altered.)

The client enters the office and I ask her to be seated. I then proceed with:

Step 1: Collect routine data.
THERAPIST: What is your name?
CLIENT: Jeri Thatcher.
T: How old are you?
C: Forty-six.
T: Your address?
C: 10 Maple Avenue.
T: Phone number?
C: 661-0011.

T: Husband's name?
C: Ronald.
T: Where does he work?
C: He runs a store in town.
T: Do you work outside the home?

(Notice how I phrased the question. Don't ask a woman whether she works—not in this day and age. If she has anything on the ball, she'll respond with a heap of indignation and say, "Of course I work.")

(I ask this question to determine whether she has a *paying* job because this often changes the leverage the woman can use in solving her problems. Employed women are usually not so dependent on their mates as those who work only as housewives. And this added independence gives them power you may want to call upon to bring about changes in the family.)

C: No, I'm a homemaker.
T: Your husband's business phone?
C: 661-5432.
T: If I need to call and can't get you at home, is it all right if I call your husband?

(Maybe she hasn't told him she's come to see me and doesn't want him to know. To let the cat out of the bag could create ill feelings.)

C: Certainly you can call him. I told him after our last argument I was going to talk to you.
T: Fine. Any children at home?

(Get a good picture of the home early in the counseling process. A woman who has no children at home has a vastly different set of frustrations from one who has four children at home plus an adult relative to care for.)

C: My two children are away at college and one son is at home.

Step 2: Determine the problem.
T: How may I help you?
C: My husband loses his temper too easily. He just can't

seem to control it and has always been that way. When he gets violently angry I don't say a thing. I clam up and take the torrent of words and swearing and things that he really doesn't mean to say. But he doesn't try to control it. So I take it but then I get bitter and angry and resentful and quiet for two or three days. Finally it goes away. I feel it's silly to go on like this, and then, when I am quiet, of course he is too. Our business, or friends, or our son who still lives at home, will bring us together and we will start talking again. Sometimes it will go for several days and things will be fine, but many times the things that he gets angry at are just so trivial. Just an impatient look can start things off.

T: If you do that or if he does?

C: I do that and then he will just fly into a tirade. I have tried so hard when he gets angry to sit back with a smile and let it roll off my back and think that words can't hurt and show him that I am not going to get angry. He gets mad in a hurry because he can't help that seemingly, but then maybe in an hour or two or three he is just almost back to normal and trying to be nice again.

(The client has gotten right to the point. This appears to be a simple case of a woman no longer wanting to tolerate an objectionable habit of her husband: his anger. A few probing questions are now in order.)

Step 3: Ask questions.

T: And you haven't gotten as angry this time as you have in the past?

C: No, because I realize that words can't hurt and it is me that gets angry. I have just got to let it roll off and I have tried to do that. You can see that I read your book on anger.

T: Have you told him that he's the one who makes himself angry and he is acting like a child because he thinks he has to have his way?

C: No. I haven't mentioned it yet. Should I?

T: Maybe. Tell me more about your husband.

C: He's very good and very generous. I can come and go as I want. He never says, "Don't buy this, don't buy that." I can do as I please with money. I think I use good reason as to what we can afford or can't. It isn't that he's all bad. It's just when he has these violent temper tantrums that I'm hurt and carry the resentment and anger. Sometimes I almost think it's hatred, but it isn't at all. We've had lots of good times together and we still will.

Step 4: Select a problem.

(The session is moving quickly. There is no need to waste time. We can proceed at once to a problem: trying to change her tactics so that his angry behavior will not continue to be reinforced.)

T: All right, could I suggest, therefore, that in the future you do a couple of things. First of all, let's start teaching him that he makes himself angry and that you don't. You may frustrate him but that doesn't have to anger him unless he *makes* himself angry over it by thinking that he *has* to have his way and that you have no right to be a human being who can frustrate him. That's absolutely absurd. As a human being you are going to be mistaken sometimes in your behavior and there is never a time when you won't be imperfect, you see?

C: Of course.

T: And so where does he get off demanding that you be perfect and never, never frustrate him again? That would be very nice, but it is totally unrealistic.

C: Another thing, I am not the only one to whom he blows up. He does it to anybody he gets frustrated with: business people and our son. My husband will blow up at Rocky just like he will at me. And Rocky is a person just like I am who takes it and seldom answers back. Then he just stews inside and sometimes for days won't talk. And that's hard for me too because I am kind of between the devil and the deep blue sea. I can see Rocky's side. I can see my husband's side. I love them both and I'm just caught.

T: But still it comes down to the fact that he doesn't know anything about his own anger. He thinks that people make him angry and you haven't taken the trouble to confront him with that nonsense.

C: Right.

Step 5: Formulate the dynamics.

(In this case the dynamics are easily determined. Her husband, for reasons not fully understood yet, thinks he has to have his way in matters of obedience from his son, his wife, and his customers. In the past he has controlled his anger in front of his customers but then ventilated his feelings to his wife. His perfectionistic aspirations for his son have made him sensitive to the young man's errors, an act his wife is no longer willing to tolerate. Why she is making her move now is not yet clear but probably stems from her middle-aged maturity.

(Having a full understanding of his dynamics is not essential for counseling to continue.)

Step 6: Educate the client.

(This is the moment when education truly starts. And the session is not yet half over.)

T: All right, now I would suggest that you talk to him and tell him just how absolutely wrong he is and stop allowing this man to make you angry. Every time you give in to him and become quiet and don't confront him with this he simply gets stronger in that habit. If you want that habit to stop, you had better do something about it instead of simply sulking about the fact that he is unkind and inconsiderate. Face him with it and say: "This is what you are doing. I don't care what you think. If you want to explode again, go ahead and explode. I am not going to get angry with you because I would be playing the same game you are. But I am not going to just sit here and just let you think somehow that I am responsible for your anger. I am not. And if you keep up this nonsense, I will just leave the room, or I will go out, or something."

C: I have done that a time or two . . . just gotten so mad down underneath, not said anything but just got in the car and gone someplace for a few hours. I just wanted to get off by myself.

T: Yes, well, I think sometimes it is important to show him that you are not going to tolerate it and say: "Look, if you want to act badly or act like a child, do it by yourself. I'll go for a walk but I am not going to sit here and take this. You can think what you want and get as disturbed as you want. But that is not my problem. That's yours." You see?

C: Yes, well—

T: And you can do that in a very firm way. You haven't been firm with him.

C: No, I haven't.

T: Okay, then how do you expect him to change?

C: I don't know. I just thought it was the path of least resistance for me to keep quiet rather than to try to argue and make him angry.

T: That's right but you see you are not disciplining yourself to overcome the problem. You think it is easier to avoid a difficult problem (which in this case is to confront your husband) than it is to face it. No, it is easier to face it. Had you faced it five years ago (if you had known what to do), you might be over it by now. Now you have a good tough year and a half, maybe, or two years of continually retraining this man until he learns how to control his anger, if you can do it at all. You may eventually have to send him in to see me, or to see somebody else, or get him to read a book on anger, or get him to attend another seminar when it comes along so that he gets educated.

C: I wish so much he would, but I didn't even suggest that because I knew he wouldn't do it. It isn't that this happens all the time, but as we are getting older why should we live with this frustration? Why can't we both just get along better? Instead, his violent temper has gotten worse in the past few years because the business seems to drive him to it. More tension, more frustration.

T: No, no, the business doesn't drive him to it. Don't tell me that the man who runs General Motors is necessarily angry because something goes wrong. With corporations that size something is going wrong all the time and they don't lose a few thousand dollars either. They literally lose millions of dollars and I am sure there are executives at that level who simply don't get angry a great share of the time. Isn't that possible? And what about the President of the United States? That kind of person can, I am sure, at times be pretty cool under some rather devastating circumstances. They know how to do it and so can your husband.

C: Well, that's my biggest problem, just to know how to cope with his extremely hot temper and impatience. He is so impatient. He'll tell me something at work, to do this, or figure this way and that way, and so on. I have a general idea as to what he means, but before I send out a letter and do it incorrectly I would say, "How do you mean I should do it? Like this?" And just like that he is angry because I didn't catch on immediately even though he didn't explain it in detail.

T: Why don't you just take the letter out of the typewriter and say: "Here. Type it yourself."

C: He doesn't type.

T: That's fine. Until he can, you can say: "Listen, when you can calm down and give me instructions without all this anger, I'll listen. In the meantime I am going to go across the street and have a cup of coffee. Now what do you think about that?" What is he going to do, fire you?

C: It would be kind of difficult.

T: Right.

C: I guess I wouldn't care. I don't have to work. I just work because I enjoy it and I know the business and we are in it together.

T: Don't you see how you are tolerating it?

C: How?

T: You are standing there and letting this man scream at you like he is your daddy and you are a little girl and you have to quake because Daddy might not like what you are doing. This is nonsense. What are you, a little girl? You are a mature woman. You're not five years old, or ten, or fifteen, but you are acting like that around your husband.

C: Yes. I realize that.

T: Well, can't you stop that?

C: It's so hard to. How could I do it? When he gets angry I am used to not saying anything.

T: But that's why he does it.

C: Once in a while I said: "I'm sorry. I didn't mean to do it." But he is still angry.

T: Because he thinks he is king of the hill, he thinks he is Napoleon and everything that he wants he has to have. Why do you perpetuate such a ridiculous philosophy in this man? Why do you continually let him go through life thinking that if he doesn't get what he wants, it's truly horrible and that you need to feel sorry for him?

C: I guess that's it.

T: When you don't get your way, do you get angry all the time?

C: No.

T: Why don't you?

C: Well, I just think it isn't that big a deal in the first place.

T: To him it is because when he doesn't get his way he thinks it's a catastrophe. He thinks it's the end of the world. And you don't. When you get frustrated sometimes you can keep your cool and act like a mature person. What makes you think he can't?

C: Because he hasn't for all these years. I guess I just think it would be impossible to change him. But I am sure he could change. In some ways he is very kind and considerate and I am more than willing to give in. I mean it isn't this bad all the time by any means. It's just the extreme temper tantrums that make me so unhappy and resentful and frustrated. We have taken nice trips and if I want to go someplace that's fine. He doesn't care at all. I can do as I please and we have a lot of good times and a good life. But it's just the anger.

T: Yes, and it is an anger which you have put up with and tolerated and not done anything to change.

C: Yes. I guess that's right.

T: And it is because you have been treating him as if he were a superior person and you a scared little girl. It is time you began to talk like a wife who is his equal and who is not going to stand around and watch Daddy scold his little girl. Right?

C: Many times I feel that down underneath he has an inferiority complex. He shouldn't but I just think when he feels this inferiority complex he tries to cover it up with his anger and shouting and swearing.

T: What has that to do with anything? I don't care why he's got it. It makes no difference why he gets angry. He still thinks that whatever has gone wrong *must* be corrected. He thinks he *has* to have his way in everything. He doesn't. And he is not going to get it.

C: Now he doesn't drink heavily at all but sometimes maybe just a little too much. I remember one night not too long ago I waited and waited for supper. He came home and I said, "I was beginning to worry." Not, "Where have you been?" I don't think I said ten words and he just blew into a rage. You'd think I had bawled him out.

T: But you see when he flies into a rage I know exactly what you do. You become apologetic. You become silent as though you have done something wrong and are implying: "I agree with you, honey. I am sorry that I have disturbed you. Yes, I am responsible for your upsets and I am sorry that I raised the question." Instead, you could say: "What is the matter with you? I asked a civil question and I expect a civil answer. You don't have to act like a child because you have something on your mind. I've got things on my mind too. I don't act like that because somebody is bugging me when I don't feel like being bugged. Grow up, man, grow up!" Can't you talk to him that way?

C: It would be hard to do.

T: Well, you'd better start.

C: I'll have to try it. It will be hard because I have never— I can never answer anybody back.

T: That's part of your training. You just haven't done it. Try a little bit o it, a little bit at a time. Assert yourself. Do your homework everyday. Try to assert yourself to your neighbors, your family, your husband, the people in your office. Start saying, "No," once in a while or start giving an order.

C: I did Sunday. At our church I had been appointed the chairman of a committee and I didn't want to do it. I'm just not good at it and I didn't want to. I fussed over it in my mind for a couple of weeks. I thought about it and I thought I am just going to walk right up and give them the list of names back and say, "I just don't want to be chairman." And I did! And I felt sort of good about it. They asked if I was opposed to the idea of this committee project and I said: "Not at all. I just don't want to be chairman." And that's pretty good for me.

T: See, you can do it when you put your mind to it. The more you practice this the smoother it gets and the bigger the issues you can eventually confront. Your husband may be one of the bigger issues.

C: The biggest one I have ever taken on, believe me. I just can't imagine that I would feel like saying all that.

T: You'll be surprised at how quickly and easily you may get him to keep quiet and respect your views. You say right now, "Well, he is going to be violent with me." But he may be more of a lamb than you think. But you won't find out until you begin to test him. I've known men who were very blustery and loud at first. They looked like they would never give an inch. Yet when others confronted them and stood nose to nose with them and meant business they often backed down because they realized they had been wrong or had too much to lose.

C: Sometimes he will do it in front of other people, such as our son or another lady in our office. That hurts worse than ever: being chewed out and raked over the coals in front of somebody else. I just wouldn't have the nerve to speak back to him then. I just don't say a word.

Step 7: Summary and quiz

(It is now time to wrap things up. A lengthy summary is not necessary. We have covered the matter well enough for the first visit.)

T: That is why you get more of it. If he can do that to you, you can do that to him. Say this in front of others: "Listen, husband, you don't talk to me this way in front of the office or in front of other people. Understand that? If you have something to say to me, call me into the office." Handle a scene that way one day and let's see what he does then. It may be the last time he ever does that to you. But you had better take the risk. Are you willing to take some risks?

C: Yes. That's why I came here, to get advice on what to do.

T: Fine. Let me summarize a moment before we close. Your husband has been trained by you over many years to have his way. You haven't confronted him until now and that's why things are getting extra tense lately. Do you understand that?

C: Yes, I think so.

T: Please tell me what I've been trying to teach you.

C: That I'd better stand up to him if I want us to be happy again.

T: And why does he get angry anytime?

C: Because he wants his way all the time?

T: No, that's not why. He thinks he *has* to have his way, not just want it.

C: Yes, I understand.

Step 8: Assign homework.

T: Now I am going to suggest that you start asserting yourself at least once a day. Stop being so afraid and start teaching him how he gets his way.

Step 9: Schedule future appointments.

T: In the meantime I won't be able to see you for about a month, but I want you to make an appointment for when I get back and I would also like you to take some psychological testing. I want to see how fragile or how strong you might be so I know just how fast I might be able to push you. Okay?

C: All right.

(Note also that a slavish adherence to these nine steps is hardly recommended. You will find that from time to time steps may be placed in different sequences or deleted entirely. Homework assignments may not always be appropriate at the end of the first visit. A summary and quiz may become superfluous if the main points of the lesson have already been repeated sufficiently during the prior portion of the session itself.)

Chapter 3

Later Sessions

In my experience through the years as a practicing therapist I have found techniques which are perhaps not emphasized enough in the literature but which are enormously important nonetheless. I want to share these insights with you.

IMPORTANT TECHNIQUES

1. Frequently remind the client of the progress that has been made.

I shall never forget my second interview with a subject whom I had previously counseled for smoking. She had been smoking two packs a day. At the second session I asked her how she was doing and she promptly told me she had failed. She had smoked three cigarettes since our last visit.

Can you imagine that? She actually thought therapy had failed because my pointers on self-discipline had not given her 100 percent control. The fact that she reduced her weekly smokes from two hundred eighty cigarettes to three apparently had no bearing on the problem for her.

This happens also with practically every other emotional problem. Clients cannot or will not regard change as significant unless it is stupendous. Therefore, point out often how well the clients have done. Constantly remind them how far they have come. When one protests, "I did better last week," point out that progress has been made in spite of the regression. Just because one hasn't achieved the next goal hardly means there haven't been important gains.

Clients and counselors alike have trouble seeing progress when it exists, because they define it too narrowly. I define progress in three ways. Any improvement in either of these three dimensions is improvement. Let's consider the symptom of anger.

We learn upon inquiry that our client is actually angry, bitter, sarcastic, or violent several times a week and that his wife is ready to leave him unless he gets control of this emotion.

Furthermore, we also learn upon inquiry that when he gets angry he stays mad for hours. He repeats his complaints, yells at the top of his voice, and when he needs to accentuate a point he will pick up a chair and smash it.

The above description can be subdivided into three dimensions: frequency, intensity, and duration. For instance, we see that the average *frequency* of his anger is several episodes a week. The *intensity* of his anger ranges all the way from sarcasm to smashing furniture. And the *duration* of his anger is often an hour or longer. Quite a fellow to live with, wouldn't you say?

In counseling we usually find that the frequency of tantrums diminishes fairly rapidly. He usually makes every effort to let the little frustrations go by even if he only suppresses them rather than talks himself out of them.

I call it progress if he comes to me during an early visit and reports that he broke the living room window, that he was angry all day, but that this was his fourth tantrum in five weeks. The anger has not reduced in intensity or in duration. But it has reduced in frequency. And this can be brought to the client's attention.

Or if he was still angry three times a week, and would stay angry for hours but now does not smash things, that's progress and had better be recognized.

2. Don't be afraid of creating dependency problems by doing a few favors.

I know of very few bugaboos in the therapy business that are as erroneous as this one. The fear of making a client dependent upon us is a legitimate one certainly, but it is highly overrated. First of all, I find that most clients are not happy to become dependent and frequently will bring this up as one of their own concerns. Secondly, most counselors are astute enough about counseling to realize that you don't make people strong by letting them lean on you indefinitely. Therefore, in my own experience I have found that although people have leaned upon me for months, it was always because they simply needed my guidance for whatever time it took before they got the strength to leave me. I still view counseling as an educational process in which the student is dependent upon the teacher until such time as the student can function without help. Only rarely, not usually, will the students be so dependent upon our strengths that they never make the break. It is therefore safe to assume that in the vast majority of cases your clients will not develop a neurotic dependency upon you but will leave you the first chance they feel able, and will be happy to save money and energy as well.

For this reason I do not hesitate to write letters for my clients, make phone calls for them, suggest jobs they might get. I will even call up lawyers, physicians, or business people on their behalf. And frequently I do this during the session itself. Such moves are especially important when the client is the weakest and needs to have something done to get things moving. The young housewife who continually talks about wanting to get back to college but has not yet called the registrar to find out when classes begin can be started on the road to education if you will simply pick up the phone, call the registrar, get the information, and pass it on to the client when you hang up the phone.

In this role the counselor becomes the catalyst who makes things happen just enough so that the client begins to get a spirit of hope and enthusiasm.

3. Ventilation vs. reason

What has been learned can be unlearned. It may take time, understanding, and great self-discipline, but it can practically always be done if those ingredients are liberally supplied.

To achieve brief therapy, this is a critical insight to accept. It requires a new view of your role and the client's role. Stop thinking of yourself as anyting but a teacher or counselor. You possess extensive knowledge in human dynamics and your client presumably does not. Your task is to show how your client is talking himself or herself into an upset and with patience and sureness show how to avoid that in the future.

This similarity between brief RET therapy and education justifies the long talks the therapist often goes into. Be directive, debate actively, accept objections and criticisms, and aim to give the client a new view of life just as a teacher does for a student.

But what about the experiential dimension? Am I suggesting that feelings are insignificant in therapy while reason alone is important? By no means. However, the experiential episode too often only makes the client feel good. The middle-aged woman who was badly treated as a girl and who is now sobbing bitterly as she recalls with great anguish memories she has relived throughout the years will not *be* better as the result of the ventilation. She will only *feel* better for a time and will soon slip into her same rage or depression as she thinks back on her youth.

However, ventilation as an aspect of the experiential dimension is enormously important because it gives you a feeling for the intensity of the problem. It also helps build rapport between client and therapist. "Can he understand my suffering?" she asks. If you can be in touch with her pain, she can open up and relate more deeply. If you fail to understand her need to either test you or relieve her pressures, you will lose her as I once did with a female client whom I was trying to help too rapidly. I glossed over her sobbing and went straight for the irrational ideas. She didn't have the vaguest notion of what I was talking about.

Now that I have conceded that feelings are important and

must be heeded, let me quickly insist that only so much ventilation and experiencing in the therapy session is necessary or helpful. When all is said and done, emotional disturbances are caused at point iB, the irrational beliefs we have, not the treatment we received. That is why it becomes a waste of time to focus endlessly on *how the client feels,* when actually it is much more fruitful to explore *how the client made and still makes himself or herself feel.* That makes sense because it helps terminate the problem rather than augment it by giving it endless attention.

I shall never forget a young lady who saw a colleague of mine and went on at great length on how she hated her mother. For a whole fifty minutes, once a week, for a period of months, this girl ranted about her mother and how she wanted her mother to roast in hell and reeled off all sorts of ingenious tortures.

I asked my colleague how she was coming along and he always assured me she was feeling great. And I had to agree with him. She left his office with a smile on her face that certainly differed from the way she looked when she came in. She even seemed serene. Then why did she have to return to therapy month after month? Simply because she was never being told how *not* to talk herself into angry states. Why wasn't she being taught? Because her therapist didn't know either.

4. Don't allow rambling.

Brief therapy is anything but nondirective. It can't afford to be. In most instances it is wasteful to let the client talk on endlessly, or ventilate for the pleasure of ventilating. True, there are times when the client has no desire to change bad habits. Therapy is an opportunity to complain, to unburden oneself, not to learn. When you feel you have such a client, try to give some instruction. Failing in this, sit back, relax, accept the inevitable, and get paid for an easy session.

However, if you can get a word in sideways, do so. Take charge of the session. Prevent rambling. You have just so much time to gather your facts and then offer information to correct behavior. Some people find it hard to be relevant. They don't know what is important to communicate. So they bounce around like a ping-pong ball from one subject to the next not knowing where to light, not even knowing what is important or how to place the issues in order of importance.

One woman recently started off her session with the complaint that she was lonely. No sooner was I about to probe into that matter than she brought up another: She was still unemployed and the prospects of a good job after graduation from college were bleak. I couldn't even ask a question about the subject before she told me about the miseries of her marriage, and how boring her husband was. Before I finally put a stop to this she wrung her hands over the thought that her term paper in English would not be finished in time.

Don't let such recitations go on. Some poor souls will use up all their time complaining and then leave your office additionally frustrated because you haven't done them any good. The fact that they might have made it all but impossible for you to get your thoughts expressed won't change their negative opinions about you.

When you sense you're dealing with one of these verbose persons, you can control the direction of the conversation fairly easily by saying: "I'm sorry to interrupt you. All that you're saying is important, I'm sure. However, could we take these subjects one at a time? Would you care to tell me more about your loneliness?"

5. Be tentative about your interpretations.

The other day I received a letter from a client I have had four sessions with already. He is bright, capable, hardworking, but not getting ahead in his career.

I made the interpretation based on fairly sound evidence that he was afraid to accept the next rung in the ladder of success because he might fall flat on his face doing so. In his letter he protested this viewpoint strongly and claimed he was being prudent at this point not to accept promotions too swiftly lest he be advanced beyond his talents.

The letter said he was depressed after our session and

would not resume therapy. I had misunderstood him seriously and therefore I couldn't be of further help.

The point is not whether I was right and he wrong. The more important issue is whether I had to push my views against a sensitive person in a dogmatic fashion when it was quickly apparent that he disagreed with me. I could just as easily have used such expressions as "I wonder if you're afraid to advance," rather than, "You must be afraid to be advanced." And I could have used such words as "perhaps," "maybe," "is it possible," "do you think," rather than "you do such and such," "you're afraid of . . . ," "you're tense over . . ."

Giving clients an option to accept or reject your interpretation is simply a matter of courtesy. Usually they will agree with you *(a)* if they aren't too defensive and *(b)* if you don't push too hard.

In some instances you'll want to be quite forceful, however, and break this rule. If you have good rapport and the interpretation is important, then press for its adoption with more than customary zeal.

Blanche was still grieving over the death of her beloved sister who died six years ago. She had pictures of the deceased all around the house. She visited her grave several times a year even though it was several hundred miles away. Sooner or later in any conversation Blanche would talk about her sister and tears would well up in her eyes.

I told Blanche she pitied herself. Indignation is a mild word to describe her shocked reaction. "Dr. Hauck! How can you say such a thing? You can't know how much I cared for my sister."

"No doubt you two were very close, Blanche. However, after six years your grieving could easily be over by now if it were a normal grieving process. When you stretch it out for six years you're either feeling sorry for yourself or for your sister."

I kept up that unswerving approach until she could get over the resistance from feelings of embarrassment. Feeling sorry for herself seemed undignified and she naturally felt defensive on this issue. I couldn't see any other interpretation that could feasibly fit the facts and that made me comfortable to be so hardheaded.

Greater caution is usually advised, however. I once counseled a couple struggling with the young husband's wavering interest in his wife. They didn't shed any light on why this was suddenly developing after three years of marriage, so I asked a few questions. I learned that they had been going steady since he was sixteen and she fifteen and that they married three years later.

I have found in these instances that infidelity may occur at such times because the man is beginning to think he has missed something by marrying early and may attempt to play catch-up.

The couple in question fit this situation to a T. The interpretation was offered, no resistance was encountered, and the session was closed with the advice to think over these conclusions until next week.

At the second session they both quickly told me how wrong I was and then proceeded to tell me what was really troubling them: he was an obsessive-compulsive personality who switched off lights around the house when they weren't actually needed, and checked the locks on the windows and doors at least three times before retiring. She was a more casual person and was being driven to distraction by his picayunish ways. When she couldn't keep every crumb off the floor and account for every cent she spent he was intolerant and ready to leave.

After a number of such sobering experiences I have found it wiser to make my interpretations more tentative than certain. I have less egg on my face as a result.

6. Perform postmortems frequently.

A mother comes to you and reports that she was not able to follow your advice the whole preceding week and that the time she spent since her last visit was wasted. This woman needs a postmortem. Although it is too late to correct the mistakes she made during the week, it is not too late to benefit by them.

In order to prevent the client from losing courage I would not hesitate to tell her that we are going to go over the past week so that we can understand what happened even though rehashing it does nothing to change it. The damage is done, but the benefits to be derived from the experience are still valuable.

I would then tell her to give me an example of a time when she had, let us say, difficulties with her children minding her. She would then explain an incident and I would quiz her as to what happened that caused the whole thing to get out of hand. I would then comment on each of her misconceptions and go over again *how* she upset herself, *what* she said to herself to do that, and what she *could* have said or done that might have corrected it.

Although this postmortem is taking place a week too late, it is important that it be done, nevertheless, because the next time she encounters this problem she may be able to understand her errors in seven hours' time rather than seven days. If she benefits from that postmortem, she will find that the time it takes to understand how she was inefficient next time may be much less. I assure my clients that the day can certainly arrive if they work hard enough on their problems when they can begin to understand the whole neurotic process *as it is taking place.* In doing so, they can literally avoid expressing their disturbances because they will nip them in the bud before they are made public. This process is only the end result of a great many postmortems that took place minutes, hours, or days away from the original event. It is rehearsing mentally what went wrong that eventually allows the time span between the insight into the situation and the correction of the situation to be diminished.

Incidentally, this is another element that gives the client a great deal of self-assurance and confidence. For even though one did not do well this time, if one sees a gradual change and mastery, this leads to hope and optimism.

7. "And," "but," "because," "prove it," etc.

Get used to these words. They are invaluable in encouraging your clients to explore the personal dynamics involved in their problems. One of the primary tasks of RET counseling is to get clients to analyze what they are telling themselves about a particular frustration. Often they do not know what they are saying, or think that what is said is enough to explain their disturbance. This is frequently a mistaken notion and they could be coaxed into a further understanding of how they are upsetting themselves. One way to do this is to prod continually with "but," "and," "because," and similar words.

For example, when a client says that he is depressed because his girl friend has rejected him, you naturally inquire in this way:

THERAPIST: What did you say to yourself that depressed you?

CLIENT: That she wouldn't see me anymore.

T: And?

C: That I felt like a chump.

T: Because?

C: Because I'm second best and I want to get even with her for rejecting me.

T: But?

C: But I won't because I still love her.

T: I see. What else did you tell yourself besides her not seeing you anymore?

C: That I don't like being without a companion.

T: And?

C: I'm going to be very lonely.

T: And?

C: I'm going to be miserable.

T: That's probably true. *But* what are you telling yourself that is making you miserable?

C: I just told you.

T: No you haven't. You've only told me *(a)* that you don't like being rejected, *(b)* that you'll feel lonely because of that rejection, and *(c)* that the loneliness is going to hurt you.

C: That's right, that's exactly what I've been saying.

T: True, but that doesn't tell me how you made yourself depressed.

C: Why doesn't it?

T: Because all those things are true, logical, or rational.

C: Of course they are. So what?

T: Then they can't upset you.

C: How's that?

T: You cannot be made upset by rational thinking, only irrational thinking.

C: I'll buy that.

T: Then why don't you tell me what you said or thought that caused you to be depressed?

C: I already did. I told you I was rejected and didn't like it, that I would feel more and more lonely and that I would feel hurt.

T: Exactly. And each of those statements is true. They cannot explain your disturbance. To do that we want to find out what the *irrational* thought is that creates your depression.

C: You mean those things I just mentioned can't upset me?

T: That's right.

C: Then what does?

T: The things you tell yourself *about* those conditions.

C: Such as?

T: Figure it out yourself. Let me give you the sane thoughts you have and let you finish them off by supplying the irrational conclusion.

C: Okay.

T: Start with your first thought.

C: I have been rejected.

T: That's right, you have been rejected. Therefore that is a correct statement. Go on and give me the irrational thought you have about it.

C: That if I am rejected, I'll surely be lonely.

T: That's not irrational either. Of course you'll be lonely. Again that's a correct statement and as such cannot explain your depression.

C: Then what about my conclusion to those first two thoughts, namely, that I'll feel miserable if I'm lonely?

T: That's probably true too. I fully expect you to feel hurt if you're lonely. Therefore that thought too cannot explain your depression. We're still looking for the irrational belief but haven't found it yet. When we do you'll know what to challenge.

C: Well, you've got me. I always thought being rejected had to depress you.

T: Because?

C: Because it just does, that's why.

T: How?

C: I don't know how, I only know it does.

T: Prove it.

C: How can I prove it?

T: I don't think you can. *You*'re saying rejection hurts. Since you believe it so strongly, prove it.

C: All right. Everybody gets hurt when rejected. There's your proof.

T: That's not true. Don't tell me you have never taken a rejection calmly. And don't tell me that a dozen men whom your girl friend may have rejected would all react as you did.

C: No, I guess not.

T: Then your argument won't hold water. But you're not convinced yet, are you?

C: No, I'm not.

T: Then tell me what else you're saying, "I get upset when I'm rejected because . . . ?"

C: Because it proves I'm worthless. Is that sensible? After all, if there weren't something wrong with me, she might have continued loving me.

T: Does that mean you have to be perfect before you think you're worthwhile?

C: Sounds like that, doesn't it? And I certainly can't be perfect, can I?

T: Not in this lifetime you can't. Go on, what else are you telling yourself about rejection hurting?

C: Beats me.

T: Then let me pull all this together for you. You started out saying three sensible things to yourself which you thought depressed you but they didn't. Your conclusions about those three conditions, however, did hurt. What were those statements? That you are worthless as a human being if you aren't loved by your girl friend. You think rejection hurts and that her loving or not loving you makes you worthwhile or worthless. Those are the irrational ideas which depress you.

C: But that's not different from what I was saying.

T: Sure it is. You said you didn't like being rejected. And I agree that was very sensible. After all, why would you enjoy rejection? But then you concluded that *(a)* it hurt to be rejected (which was incorrect) and *(b)* you were worthless for being rejected (also not true). Those two conclusions, that rejection proves you are a nothing and that it has to hurt to be a nothing are completely false. You can't prove they make sense. So why believe them?

C: I'll sure have to give this a lot of thought.

T: I agree. Give it a lot of thought because . . . ?

C: Because I want to understand myself better.

T: Because . . . ?

C: So I can get over being depressed?

T: Right, so you can talk yourself out of this and future depressions.

8. Set expectations for continuing counseling.

You may be surprised to find at the conclusion of your initial session, or any session for that matter, that your client is ready to terminate. Unless you have been making some statements alluding to your hope that the sessions will continue and further education is needed you will find some resistance to this idea.

Therefore, I find it helpful to prepare my client for continued work on the problem by assigning certain tasks, not always actual homework assignments, but simply tasks such as thinking about the problem some more or thinking over the things we have talked about in the session. I expect the client to get a better hold on the problem and report back to me on another visit.

In this way the client learns that I do not think that we are through with counseling, that work is expected between sessions, and that I expect there will be another session. And I find that there is less resistance when there is some preparation for this before the end of the session.

This subtle technique can often mean the difference between success and failure in getting a client to come back for needed consultations. It is not a way of filling in your schedule and making money. It is a way of encouraging the client to be realistic and to recognize that additional work is often needed to overcome bad habits. In fact, many problems are habits and bad habits frequently require a great deal of concentrated effort to change. In this way I avoid the derogatory term of neurosis. This the client can live with much easier. When I say, "Go home and work on those bad habits and see if you can replace them with healthier habits," the client seems to be more willing to do so.

9. Make notes during each session.

There were many years of my practice during which I would take an initial interview, perhaps do some testing, and hardly ever make another note in the folder unless I thought it was important for a court case or I was recording termination of therapy.

I thought it was not my responsibility to remember from week to week what the person's problem was. I felt that was the client's responsibility. In a way I still think so. However, I have changed my practice about note-taking for several reasons.

First, for a clinical psychologist at least, the peer review committees of the psychological associations are becoming more commonplace and we had better know what we did at a certain time so that we can testify to our behavior. Having a complete set of notes is also important when you appear in court as an expert witness. It does not sound as though you

have done your homework, or that you are much of a professional if you have one single sheet in your folder after having
seen a client many times and you are trying to bring back
from memory all the important details.

Also occasionally, by having notes available to me, I can
refresh my memory on points I might have forgotten, or can
correct the client's memory when a statement is made with
which I disagree.

Another reason I do this is that I accept reality, even if it
happens to be unfair. Though I could get by reasonably well
without having notes, as I did for many years, I found much
objection on the part of my clients when I could not recall
details concerning their lives. I decided to give in, and now
have my secretaries pull out the folder each time the person
comes. This allows me to glance over my notes quickly to
ascertain what the problem is. This indeed goes over a great
deal better than merely asking them how they have been. Too
often I did not know from the answer what the clients were
referring to and the puzzlement showed on my face. They
frequently felt I had no interest in them if I didn't remember
from an earlier time what we had talked about. Despite my
assuring them that I would remember their case well and
fully if they simply would give me a few details to go on, I
did not console them greatly. It is primarily for this reason
that I now have my folders in front of me even though it takes
extra secretarial time, and even though, in principle, I don't
think it is my responsibility. However, the benefits from improved relationships with the clients outweigh the little inconvenience it causes. The notes are particularly useful in
checking on the progress of the homework assignments.
You're not likely to remember all your recommendations
unless you list them.

Furthermore, when you come across an issue you want to
explore farther, it helps greatly to put that fact in your notes.
At your next session you can glance at the capital letter *R*
in the left-hand margin (it stands for Recommendations) and
immediately pursue the unfinished business you could easily
have forgotten.

10. Encourage debate.

Too often for my tastes clients will apologize for wanting to make a suggestion as to their own case. They humbly admit that they are "not psychologists or analysts and they hope they don't sound like one but . . ."

These people miss entirely the nature of a counseling relationship. It is a teacher-student arrangement and as such permits debate, discussion, speculation, and questioning. The very nature of the counseling relationship, the very nature of good mental health rests largely upon getting one's facts straight, getting one's thinking correct, and then applying it in everyday life. A client who is unwilling to raise a question and put objections to the test is not likely to be convinced of anything. The way to be convinced of an idea is to subject it to the most intense criticism it can stand. If it survives, the idea has greater credibility than it had before.

For this reason I strongly encourage my clients to question me about anything I say or anything which RET espouses. I urge them never to feel sheepish about their protestations since what they do not question they are not likely to accept. It is wrong to accept these ideas on blind faith because they are too likely to crumble unless they are grounded in the solid earth of reason. When a client will not or does not raise speculations and questions I sometimes do this for him.

"Why can we not judge ourselves by our behavior? Why are a person and the person's actions not the same? Do I truly mean it when I say that no one should blame oneself for anything?" These are the kinds of questions I will pose when I think a client has those in mind but does not express them. And in this way we can continue our debate. I am happy to report that I win most of the debates and you should also if you want to be a successful and healthy counselor.

11. Is the client listening?

In RET counseling you will find that there are stretches at a time when you have to do quite a bit of talking. This is for your client's benefit and it is important that those mini-sermons be heard. I sometimes find that the client is trying to listen respectfully but not listening at all, and I am wasting my breath. This may be because I am going on too long, or because the client does not see the importance of what I have to say, or disagrees with me but doesn't want to tell me so and is just waiting for me to end my speech so we can get on to something else.

You can notice this condition of disinterest in several ways. First of all, if the client starts looking around the room rather than at you, that means you have lost attention and you had better get back to that problem rather than the one you are immediately talking about.

Secondly, the client answers your comments with an irrelevant question, or makes an irrelevant comment and starts on another issue entirely. The client hasn't been listening.

And thirdly, the client tells you after you have presented a complex idea for the first time that it is perfectly clear and completely understood. You can be fairly sure that not a thing is clear or understood.

Whenever these conditions exist I try to interpret to the client that these ideas are strange and different, and that they challenge completely everything one has been taught in the past. The likelihood of disregarding them is great. Therefore to see if they are understood I ask, "Would you care to comment on the point I just made?" In this way we learn very quickly what has been absorbed or ignored.

I also caution the client that many of the ideas that I will be giving simply take time to absorb. As foolish and outlandish as they may sound at times I do not want them dismissed as so much nonsense. If necessary, I can challenge with questions such as these: "If you knew this material all along, then why were you upset in the first place? If you heard it before, obviously you did not believe it?" And then we can go into an examination of what the problem seems to be at that point.

12. Learn when to terminate counseling.
The termination question is a needless one. It implies that

the problem has been resolved, that no further counseling is necessary from that day forward, and that you might as well terminate the relationship because no more education is needed.

I prefer to think of termination as a provisional event rather than a final one. To me termination means that the person will not come back for a time but that the door is always open so that counseling can be resumed at any time it is wanted. There is no such thing as a totally knowledgeable person or a totally stable one. Life always has surprises around the corner for all of us, and we never know from year to year when we are going to need additional help.

Keeping this provisional definition of termination in mind, I find that there are two conditions that justify termination.

The first is when the client is obviously better, has improved a great deal, and both of you feel that a cessation of the current therapy sessions can take place.

The second condition for termination is when the person has no interest in learning. You have tried to motivate without success. The client does not agree there is a problem and therefore there is nothing worth working on. The sensible thing to do is to terminate. Say that you are willing to try it at another time when help is wanted. Alcoholics who will not accept help have to hit bottom first. The fellow who will not treat his wife more kindly may have to be divorced first, and perhaps even more than once, before he realizes he has a problem that requires professional attention.

The counselor is cautioned not to take termination too seriously when it occurs prior to improvement. This happens to all of us no matter how good we are. People will avoid therapy for the same reasons they avoid education of any kind. Some don't want to work as hard as is required. Others aren't in enough pain yet to motivate them for counseling. Others think headshrinkers ought to have their heads examined, while a percentage are afraid of what they'll find out.

And we're supposed to hold ourselves responsible for every client we can't help? Not on your couch I won't. We goof up from time to time, certainly. But let's not accept blame for the terminations for which we had no fault whatever.

A TYPICAL BRIEF COUNSELING SESSION
(Abridged)

(I saw this nineteen-year-old woman several years ago and was able to treat her depression quickly. She required therapy on two other occasions in the four years I was able to follow her, although not for the symptom for which she first sought me out—depression.)

THERAPIST: Yes, speak. (I'm being facetious.)

CLIENT: I don't know what to say other than that I am depressed.

T: Okay. What are you depressed about?

C: Well, number one, my act broke up. And, number two, about three weeks ago the guy I had been going with for a year all of a sudden decided that was it.

T: Yes.

C: I just don't have any sense of direction. I've got a good job and I have been working for a year. I have ups once in a while but most of the time I have downs. I lost ten pounds in three weeks and I get about three or four hours' sleep a night. I've tried everything. All my close friends tell me to take every day at a time, take it easy, and just be happy. It's easier said than done. I'm trying to figure out how to do it. I just don't know. I have tried everything. I have tried going out and having a good time with my friends. Last weekend I took off to the cities to see another group. I went out with an old friend. It is fun for the time but as soon as I get back and start thinking about things again, I always keep living in the past.

T: Thinking about what in particular?

C: That all of a sudden after a year Randy has gone. I mean that's all there is to it. And there are no ifs, ands, or buts, I have got to learn to accept it but I can't. It is just too hard. I have been with him since he was in the senior year of high school and I watched him mature as all of his dreams sort of fell into place.

(The problem is obvious. She is depressing herself over rejection. Probably a bad case of self-pity because she thinks that she has to be loved and that rejection has to hurt. Though we are only a few minutes into the session, we can proceed to educate her already as to how she is doing this to herself. I can proceed to show her the three ways she could be hurting herself.)

T: So what do you think is depressing you now?

C: Just a lack of being able to get my head where I think it should go. I wish I knew what I could do about it.

T: May I suggest something? I'll tell you about depression. I'll tell you the ways in which people get depressed and then you tell me what you are doing. All right? We'll see if we agree.

There are essentially three different ways that I know of by which people become depressed. The first is to blame themselves a great deal over their mistakes. They have done something wrong. They have behaved badly. They have committed a sin and they think it is perfectly sensible to castigate themselves, to run themselves into the ground, to hate themselves, and never forgive themselves for their errors. That would be one fine way of getting depressed.

Another way is to feel sorry for yourself. You pity yourself, when you think you have been a living doll and you have done your very best and should have all the fruits of your hard labor. But this world very unjustly does not give you what you think you deserve, and isn't that too bad? See? That feeling sorry for yourself, that self-pity is another good way to get depressed.

Now the third way is to pity someone else. You see a child with a broken leg and your heart goes out to him. Or you see someone who is blind and you are ready to cry for him. Or you see a dead dog on the highway and you are all shook up over that. Or you see a starving infant from India on TV and that breaks your heart. That will also depress you.

The point is that any of these methods can depress you. They all look the same although the reasons for the depression are different.

C: Well, as far as blaming myself for anything, I can say that I have not done anything to deserve any bad treatment for what happened. He told me so many times that I was just about the perfect girl. All I cared about was that he was happy and I was happy making him happy and vice versa.

T: Which of those methods are you using to depress yourself?

C: I don't feel sorry for anybody else. And I don't think I feel sorry for myself. I'm not sure. I don't necessarily feel sorry for myself like saying: "Oh, poor me. The whole world is down on me." That is not true. Life is fine and everything is beautiful basically. It is just that right now, I'm trying to adjust to the fact that love is a habit and all of a sudden I am on my own again completely.

(Don't believe her. Have faith in your theory. She is blaming herself, pitying herself, or pitying someone else. Just because she doesn't see it yet is immaterial.)

T: All right. Are you blaming yourself for that?

C: I don't think so.

T: All right. Are you pitying him?

C: Not at all. Randy knows what he's doing.

T: All right, then what's left?

C: Just the fact that I feel sorry for myself.

T: Do you think you feel sorry for yourself?

C: I don't think I do. There are things that I want to do. I don't know what they are and I don't know how to get to them.

T: Yes, but that's because you are depressed.

C: Well, probably.

T: When you are all out of steam and in a blue mood you have no energy and can't do a great deal about picking yourself up, can you?

C: I already know what part of my problem is. It's just that I don't know how to solve it.

T: What's that?

C: I hate being in crowds alone. That really frightens me. It is not a paranoid thing at all. It is not like everybody is watching me.

T: What kind of thing is it then?

C: It's that I have this desire to relate to everybody and get to know everybody and yet they don't necessarily want to get to know me. In a way I am terribly frustrated, I suppose. I guess I set too high a goal for myself and I always just about make it. Sometimes I make it, but then all of a sudden something happens and the bottom falls out.

T: Right. Like going after your boyfriend. You're having a nice relationship and an act going and the whole thing blows up. Right?

C: Right.

T: Now what do you suppose you are telling yourself about the fact that you are experiencing disappointments?

(Notice how vague she is. I don't want her to ramble and lose track of my target: getting her to understand her self-pity. Her fear of crowds can wait until I educate her about her hypomania and depression, especially since she's not bothered that way greatly at this time.)

T: Is it possible that you are making a big thing out of the fact that you have lost a boyfriend? Can't you see how you have probably made that into an awfully big issue?

C: Well, admittedly I am depressing myself. Everything I do to make myself happy or unhappy comes from within me first.

T: That's right.

C: If I am out for a good time and I am out for happiness, it is up to me to find it and find a person who will make me happy.

T: Okay, but do you also see that when you get depressed now that you are also talking yourself into that? It is not the breakup of a business or the loss of your boyfriend that is literally causing you to be depressed. Can you see that?

C: Well, I suppose that I am talking myself into depression.

But the only reason I am talking myself into it is because of the things that have happened recently.

T: No. You could also have these things happen to you and say entirely different things to yourself which would not depress you.

C: Yes, I can do what Randy always does when he gets down and gets uptight. He just says, "The hell with it." He has this uncanny ability of completely putting up a wall between himself and what is bugging him. I suppose I'm too emotional. I have my down moments like anybody else. But I am not constant either way.

T: There is no reason why you could not be on the light side most of the time without any danger of being depressed. All you have to do is learn how not to depress yourself. And in your case if you would learn how not to pity yourself over your reversals by making great big issues out of them, you could simply say: "Okay, so I lost a job. Big deal, maybe I will go into another act that is even better than this one." Or: "All right, so I lost my boyfriend, He is not the only guy in the whole world. I'm an attractive girl. I can get others. So why am I making such a big deal of it?"

C: But that's so hard. I could never be undisturbed over losing a boyfriend. It has to hurt.

T: No it doesn't, if you don't let it.

C: If I don't let it? How could I ever do that?

T: By not saying irrational things to yourself. You see you get upset by having upsetting thoughts, not by having frustrations. If you think depressing thoughts, you'll feel depressed. You don't get depressed by having sad things happen to you. You get depressed only when you blame yourself, pity yourself, or pity others *over* sad things.

C: Then you're saying Randy's leaving me didn't make me depressed?

T: That's right. You depressed yourself by telling yourself that it was terrible to lose Randy and that because you didn't want that to happen, the world should treat you fairly and not let it happen.

C: And what's so wrong with that?

T: Because those thoughts are illogical, they don't make sense.

C: What's so foolish about getting upset over losing a loved one?

T: For one thing, it hurts to get upset. Secondly, it's a pain that you bring on by yourself. Thirdly, it does nothing about bringing back the loved one. You cannot prove that it will be catastrophic if Randy does not love you again. Yet you insist you will never be happy again because your life is over.

C: What would you suggest I do?

T: Talk to yourself in a different way. *Debate* with yourself. Thoroughly *question* the idea that life is pointless without Randy. *Analyze* the idea that rejection has to hurt. When you have an irrational thought just don't let it sit there and eat away at your emotional control. Counteract each false idea with a sensible idea and you'll surely feel better in a hurry.

C: Well, . . . what are some sensible ideas I could give myself?

T: You could convince yourself, for instance, that you need food, shelter, and clothing, not Randy's love. It might be wonderful if he returned your love, but just think what would happen to you if he died. Would you die too?

C: Of course not. But I'd feel like it.

T: Granted, but you'd get over it. Furthermore, you could remind yourself that you could find a new romance. After all, if you were able to land Randy, why can't you land someone else? And how can you be sure the next romance won't be better than the last one? You have an even chance that your next love will be as good as it was with Randy.

(I am giving her a sample of the ideas she can be giving herself in the days ahead. I could continue at some length to offer argument after argument, but this is not necessary. Giving her several rational ideas she can use for the present is quite sufficient.

(The remainder of this session was spent in teaching her the ABC's of emotional disturbance.)

SECOND SESSION

T: How have you been?

C: Fine.

T: What has been happening to you?

C: I sat down when I got home from the first time I came here and said to myself: "Yes, that's what you are doing. You are feeling sorry for yourself." I just sat there and thought about it for a while. Then I went to sleep that night and slept nine hours and since then everything has been just great. I finally got my head together now. It's just that problems aren't bothering me anymore now. If something starts bugging me, I don't pay any attention to it, like living alone. I don't feel so lonesome anymore, because even when there aren't people around I can find things to do now. Like sewing and cooking and things like that. I just feel better.

T: Do you think this is related to the fact that you are not feeling so sorry for yourself?

C: Oh, yes, when you are feeling sorry for yourself, you just sit there and you don't feel like doing anything. There are an awful lot of things to do, but you don't feel like doing anything. Lately I have just been finding things to do like waxing my kitchen floor, which needed it anyway and I put it off. In general, I am keeping myself a lot busier. I don't have much time to sit down and mope about it. So it is nice. The boy I was going with called me up two nights after I talked to you. We sat and talked for three and a half hours and generally we are great friends and that is it. There are no hard feelings, no pain or anything. We are both content and that is great. I really feel like an individual now instead of part of someone else.

T: Well, now if you hadn't found out about your being a self-pitier would these events have affected you the same way?

C: I don't think so. If I had been depressed and somebody called me up and said, "We've got someone to join the group," I probably would have said, "All right," and I probably would not have felt too strongly either way about it. But as it happened they called me up and I was excited. It's just great.

T: Well, I am glad to hear that. You seem to have caught on very quickly. You stopped this neurotic self-pity and any good that was about to come into your life could be taken advantage of, couldn't it?

C: Yes, I had the capability of grasping it and going with it.

T: That's it.

C: Where before, I don't think I could have done anything. I would have just sat there and it would have had to fall on top of me before I realized what was happening.

T: How did you talk yourself out of being so self-pitying?

C: It was like a lead balloon being dropped on my head. It's a great awakening. That's just what it was. It just happened. I don't know how. I was sitting back watching television. My living room is my bedroom, so I was lying on the sofa and I was watching TV and it struck me. "How much time are you going to waste feeling sorry for yourself when you have so many things to do?" And that was it. I just started being myself again, which was great.

T: That is the kind of verbalizing that goes on when a person begins to challenge self-pitying attitudes. Somewhere along the line you said to yourself: "This bad thing has happened to me, but why shouldn't it? Secondly, is it really as horrible as I continually make it out to be? Thirdly, do I have to have everything I want? Is it really a terrible thing if I am not pleased constantly?" You see, somehow along the way you challenged those things too.

C: I've got problems right now, but I am not sitting around and worrying myself to death about them. I am not ignoring them either. That would be just going to the opposite extreme.

T: That's right. You want to pay attention to your problems and when you have done as much as you can about them, get your mind off them and start to live. Correct?

C: Sure, you can't do anything more than just think about

the problem and try to solve it. It doesn't have to bring you down and make you depressed because there is a problem.

T: Yes, and that is usually done by feeling sorry for yourself or blaming yourself over the problems.

C: Yes, it is one thing to feel sad when something bad happens for a time, but not to be able to pick yourself up by the seat of the pants and say, "Well, okay, let's go on to something new," was exactly the problem.

T: Okay. Now the next time you come across a reversal, an undeserved act, a mean action on the part of somebody else, what had you better be careful of so that you don't wind up in the same mess again?

C: Well, I ask myself if it is truly bad. Big deal. A lot of bad things happen to a lot of people. There are a lot of bad things in the world, but maybe you can make it better. If you sit around and worry about it, it is going to make it worse.

T: Yes, that's it. You don't have to focus on it at all times just because it is a bad thing. The more you do that, the more you become worried, tense, and nervous, and so on. Correct?

C: Right.

T: What is another thing that you can tell yourself in order to become self-pitying and depressed?

C: You mean if I were actually going to become depressed?

T: Yes. How could you do that?

C: I don't really know that I could do that anymore.

T: Well, sure you could. What have I been teaching you?

C: Yes, but if something would come along and hit me in the head that would be a real problem, I would probably say: "Get out of here. I don't want any problems." I really don't know.

T: Okay, let's talk from a theoretical point of view. How does one theoretically become self-pitying?

C: Well—

T: What must you do to yourself in order to feel self-pity?

C: How do you get depressed by self-pity? You just figure it shouldn't happen to you.

T: And, that it's awful not to have your way. In this particular kind of therapy the idea goes like this: "It is awful not to have one's way." And it was true that you didn't get your way in two instances.

C: Right.

T: One was that your group broke up and the other was that your boyfriend left you. Now in both of these cases you were saying, "I don't want this to happen and I wish I could have my way."

C: Right.

T: That's not neurotic talk. What must you add to that in order to wind up with a neurotic feeling?

C: To expect that it is not going to happen to me and it can't and it won't. So you start worrying yourself to death until you start thinking: It is happening. What am I going to do? and you can't pull yourself up.

T: Not quite. If you talk to yourself that way, you wind up nervous and jittery. What do you have to say to yourself to get depressed?

C: Okay. Just take it as it is instead of saying, "I don't deserve this happening to me." Just take it like it is. It *is* happening, so what am I going to do about it?

T: Now I want you to remember this phrase very, very clearly. This is the thing which sends you over the edge. It is the belief that it is horrible not to have one's way. Get that? And if you question that, if you challenge that with: *"Why* do I have to have everything my way? What is so terrible about not getting everything I want? Is it really so horrible? Whether it includes boyfriends, whether it includes my parents living, or my getting my career, is it really terrible and horrible and should I flip my lid over it?" That you can keep asking yourself the next time a bad thing happens.

C: I'll try to remember that.

T: Good for you. What about those symptoms you told me about? Was it three weeks ago I saw you?

C: Yes, it was about that, I think.

T: You said, as I recall, that you had lost about ten pounds and that for a brief period of time you weren't eating very well, you weren't sleeping very well.

C: I was sleeping four hours a night.

T: And you were crying a good deal of the time and so on.

C: Yes.

T: What has happened to those symptoms?

C: Well, as far as sleep goes, if I sleep very little, it is my own fault because I just don't want to go to sleep because there is something happening. It is not a matter of my trying to get to sleep and I can't. If I want to sleep now, I can sleep fine. And as far as eating, I don't know. I am still not eating a whole lot but I don't think that is emotional, I think it is that I am so busy, my mind just isn't geared toward food. But crying, I haven't really cried about anything.

T: Well, it sounds like you have done a fine job. Do you think you have to come back?

C: Well, I wouldn't really think so. What more could I do except sit around and talk about how happy I am? And that is not neurotic when you are happy.

T: Now once again before you go, what is the neurotic idea or that irrational thought which sends you or me into depression by self-pity?

C: To think that I would have to get my way and when I don't it is the worst thing that can happen to me.

T: And to get out of that feeling of self-pity, what can you do?

C: The only thing you can do is look the problem straight in the eye and say: "Okay, you are a problem but don't bother me. I've got things to do and get involved in something." That is the main thing anyone depressed should do —just really get involved in something if possible.

T: At the same time what can one do about that idea?

C: Realize that one doesn't always have to get one's way. Things just don't always have to follow the pattern one wants them to.

T: Right. And it isn't really earthshaking. It isn't going to kill us if we do not get anything we want.

C: We might sit around and feel bad about it for a while, but we should not constantly feel bad about it.

T: It is a matter of challenging that irrational idea, isn't it?

C: Right.

T: Challenge it and stop believing that nonsense and not talk yourself into feeling sorry for yourself and then you won't be depressed and feel sorry for yourself.

C: Right.

T: Okay. I congratulate you. I think you have done a very fine job.

C: I want to thank you for your help too. You gave me new ideas to think about.

T: Well, you did the work and followed the instructions very carefully. I think you worked on it hard and gave it some thought, which was necessary.

C: But I never by myself would have thought I was feeling sorry for myself. I was too clouded in my thinking to even think of that at all.

T: Well, that's why occasional counseling is a good thing, isn't it?

C: It is a good thing. It really is.

T: Okay. Go on from here and see what happens. If you need to come back for any reason at all, give me a call and we will get together. In the meantime have a nice time.

C: I certainly thank you.

(We can question the depth of her changes. Could she truly have changed so much in three weeks? Certainly. However, to be realistic we can expect her to backslide from time to time even though she is giving lip service to RET principles. For the time being, however, she has rid herself of her depressive symptoms and feels better. I suspect she can still be subject to spells of worry and anxiety, but she has not seen the need to address those issues yet.

(Though we are left with unfinished business, we have accomplished the goals of brief therapy anyway. She is functioning again, she has learned a few important psychological facts that can help her avoid self-pity in the future, and that is about all we can expect.

(This is not a flight into health, nor is it resistance. She has progressed as much as she could in two sessions and as much as was needed for her problem at this time. Does she require more therapy? Ideally, yes. For practical purposes, no. That's what brief therapy is all about and how it differs from long-range therapy.)

Chapter 4

The Best
Rational Arguments

Over the years I have observed that a large portion of my clients were distressed in four ways. I realized then that proficiency in counseling those neurotic reactions would make me a proficient therapist. I would then be able to deal comfortably on any one day with between 75 percent and 90 percent of the complaints brought to me in therapy. These frequent disorders are depression, anger, fear, and poor self-discipline. If you can master this foursome, you will be able to apply this knowledge to most age groups (including many children down to the age of five); from the bright down to the borderline mentally retarded: from university professors to the uneducated, and to those whose major difficulties stem from sexual or marital problems.

I began to sense the existence of the neurotic foursome when I was writing *The Rational Management of Children* in 1967. By the time I was writing *Reason in Pastoral Counseling* during 1970 and 1971 the division of these four conditions was quite complete. Over the following years I wrote a paperback book on each condition. First came *Overcoming Depression* in 1973, *Overcoming Frustration and Anger* in 1974, followed by *Overcoming Worry and Fear* in 1975, and I wound up with *How to Do What You Want to Do: The Art of Self-Discipline* in 1976.

These four neurotic conditions, and others related to them (self-blame, self-pity, jealousy, procrastination, perfectionism, etc.), will be discussed in the following pages, together with techniques I have found helpful in correcting them.

Since brief counseling is largely a matter of getting the client to change irrational beliefs to rational ones, those points which the counselor makes and which turn the tide in the client's thinking are most powerful tools. Learn, therefore, which arguments are ignored by clients and which are respected. Some arguments are so patently logical they are practically impossible to refute. They open new views to an issue, views the client may never have been exposed to before.

When you have made an extremely relevant comment to your client you will often recognize that you have touched a deep nerve by the way the client listens. Look at the eyes. They are intensely focused on you. There is no evidence of boredom or of self-consciousness. When you make a powerful rational rebuttal against neurotic statements, one listens as never before, not always, but often enough. It is a moment like this which Rudolf Dreikurs, the Adlerian, called the "recognition reflex" (Dreikurs, 1968).

Reason takes hold in most instances merely because it is so correct. However, it helps enormously to have a *series* of logical arguments at your fingertips which you can call upon which are so reasonable, so irrefutably right, that an opposing idea cannot exist once the rational one has been grasped.

Your strength as an RET counselor is measured in part by the ease with which you can call up rational arguments to counterattack irrational arguments. But, in addition to ease, you also seek arguments that have uniqueness, humor, and an overriding impression of correctness. The more such arguments you possess, the better counselor you will be. In any single day you will use some arguments several times, even use the same ones consecutively with several clients. No matter, life isn't always exciting. And if you cannot come up with fresh debate material, be satisfied with that which has worked well in the past.

The following remarks present those points you as counselor will want to understand fully so that you can have them at the tip of your tongue and use them when appropriate. If one logical and rational point doesn't convince the client, use another and another until you win the debate or until time runs out.

SELF-BLAME

1. The more a person blames himself or herself for unacceptable behavior, the more unacceptable behavior that person will perform. (Ellis, 1962; Hauck, 1973; Glassor, 1969; Hurlock, 1973; Meichenbaum, 1977; Phillips and Wiener, 1972)

Self-hate generates a guilt that is often soothed only by more self-punishment. One of the best ways to punish yourself is by doing more mean and negative things. This can become a vicious cycle: you injure someone in a car accident, blame yourself, feel a need to suffer, begin to drink, have another accident, etc.

2. If hate and violence are immoral, self-hate is no exception. (Beck, 1963; Kisker, 1972; Zax and Cowen, 1972)

You are no less a human than anyone else. The rules of charity and forgiveness you apply to others apply to you as well. Do not justify your self-inflicted suffering on the grounds that you should not have acted unwisely, or that what you did is somehow so much worse than the actions of others. All of us behave badly some of the time. Instead of limiting the pain that you may have brought into the world by some thoughtless act, you increase it when you add your own pangs of guilt to the stress suffered by others. That's double trouble.

3. If people are truly imperfect, it is just plain folly to believe they can behave perfectly. (Beck, 1967; Ellis, 1957, 1961; Hauck, 1972, 1973)

You are not conveniently getting yourself off the hook when you forgive yourself for your errors. You are doing the only thing that makes sense. Imperfect beings commit murder, embezzle, abuse children, rape, steal, lie, and commit a hundred assorted evils. They must sometime during their daily and weekly existence act unwisely on a small or large scale. That's what it means to be human.

4. Every major religious system existing today accepts humankind as fallible but worthy of forgiveness nevertheless. Guilt *feelings* (as distinguished from the admission of guilt) are un-Christian. (Hauck, 1972)

Though the clergy sometimes forgets this precious wisdom, forgiveness for errant behavior is a foundation stone in much religious thinking. "We're all sinners" we are repeatedly reminded, and appropriately so if by sinners we mean wrongdoers. Why, then, must we reject ourselves for behaving in ways our imperfect natures allow us to behave?

5. Self-blame distracts the person's attention from focusing on a solution to faulty behavior. (Bakan, 1962)

How could it be otherwise? Concentration and objectivity are critical in the intelligent alteration of behavior. Past mistakes must be reviewed and carefully analyzed. Techniques must be developed which allow you to detect the objectionable behavior as soon as it occurs. A plan of action that produces better behavior can then be developed. These steps, however, cannot emerge if you are focusing almost exclusively on how unworthy you are, how you ought to be horsewhipped, and that you'll never change.

6. Self-blame offers a model by which others learn to be self-hating also, thereby increasing the suffering in the world. (Block and Christiansen, 1966)

The offspring of a self-blamer are only too prone to adopt the same punishing philosophies. Children who might otherwise have escaped this needless burden soon learn to judge themselves by each imperfect or rude act and to suffer the same fate as their parents who were probably similarly conditioned as children.

Children can pick up the slightest nuances of speech. A southern child sounds like his dad, while a northern child hears those minute differences which his New England father has learned and reflects them in idiom and inflection. Is it not also obvious that behavior and thinking are also likely to be imitated in almost every particular? Depressive parents often rear depressive children.

7. It is never rational to judge oneself as a good person or as a bad person based on one's actions. (Ellis, 1961, 1966)

The human being is always much more than a combination of traits. No known number of traits has been found that satisfactorily describes the total person. All that can rationally be said about human actions are statements that express a judgment about those actions. They are not judgments about the person.

This is an immensely important distinction to make because *the separation of act from person* is precisely the best way to combat self-blame and the three emotional distresses that arise from it: guilt, inferiority, and depression.

To conclude that you, as a total human being, are worthless because your actions are mean is to go beyond the evidence. We have no guarantee that you won't improve shortly. You may have acted saintly for twenty years before committing this error. And, in any event, you behave badly not because you are intrinsically evil, but because you are *imperfect* from birth, or you are *ignorant,* or *disturbed.*

Just as you have no rational basis for blaming yourself when you do badly, you have no rational basis for praising yourself for doing magnificently. Michelangelo was not a better person than you or I, he was a better painter and sculptor.

Good behavior doesn't make good people, just people who do good. We are neither good nor bad. Our actions are good or bad in accordance with the way we look at them. But we are never good or bad, we just are. In this way we easily avoid self-hate and its opposite, vanity.

We are vain and conceited only when we believe we are better than others (as a person) because we are better at performing particular acts. Being a great artist doesn't make a person better than others (except as an artist). To insist we are the most beautiful or most intelligent persons in the world is not in itself a conceited statement. It becomes vanity only when we believe we are overall superior to others because of our beauty or intelligence.

SELF-PITY

1. Life is unfair. (Adler, 1965)

No matter how bad your situation is or how good it is for others, there is no reason why it cannot or should not be so. This world is not heaven and never will be. Therefore, you will get the shaft sooner or later: it's only a matter of time. If you don't get an unfair deal, someone else will. And that person will then have the same complaints you have.

Life will always be up and down, noble and loathesome, moral and wicked. It will make sense and not make sense. And the person who demands fairness and justice is dreaming. If they come, one is lucky. Self-pity, in view of these easily demonstrated observations of life, is totally inappropriate.

2. The benefits from self-pity are a poor trade-off for the suffering it costs. (Solzhenitsyn, 1975)

It hurts to pity yourself. Though others may weep for you and that may feel delicious, being depressed is no joke either. In addition, your mate, family, and friends will soon tire of your whining and lose respect for you. If you're not careful, you'll feel even more sorry for yourself if that happens and then your problem will get worse. No matter how seductive the pleasures of feeling sorry for yourself may be, you are almost always better off keeping a stiff upper lip, your shoulders squared, and your chest out. A thick skin is the best guarantee that life and its many stings won't bring you down. Guts, fortitude, and a thick hide are often common traits found among strong, mature, and stable people.

3. Not getting one's way is sad, not tragic. (Mintz, 1961)

To deny that life is sometimes a cross to bear is to be Pollyannish. It *is* tough. However, practically all the hurts we are sure we can't endure, we endure. We may not do this with grace and aplomb, but survive it we do. Seldom does it turn out to be the tragedy we envisioned.

If you lose a leg, that's sad, not tragic. We all know persons who are still productive, active, and happy even though crippled. This same observation is applicable to most of our woes, especially for the masses who live in the advanced countries. At our worst we still live at a level most people in Bangladesh or India or the blacks of South Africa would think was mighty fine. And even they have repeated happy moments highlighting their lives despite their miseries.

4. Self-pity leads to increasing feelings of low self-confidence. (Farberow and Shneidman, 1961)

Even though self-pitiers feel strong and secure because they have gotten others to moan and groan along with them, the fact is usually forgotten that their problems have not been mastered after all. Self-pity is a reaction to defeat. It is a complaint about a problem. After all the weeping and gnashing is over, self-pitiers still have not removed the frustration. This means they have not tested themselves. Growth proceeds through accepting challenges, living with doubt and uncertainty for a time, and perhaps coming out victoriously in the end. Self-confidence is the result of accepting that risk, studying the errors, taking that knowledge back for further trial and error until improvement is evident. This can require that hundreds or thousands of trials be necessary before progress is noted. Self-pitiers miss out on self-confidence because they do not experience this sense of mastery, this gradual sense of victory.

OTHER-PITY

1. Neither the other-pitier nor the person being pitied is benefited by the well-meant suffering. (Hauck, 1973)

As noble as the other-pitier's intention may be, other-pity is like an insidious drug that leaves the user less capable of dealing with life. From whence is friend or family member supposed to derive strength after the other-pitier demonstrates so clearly that adversity will prevail? If someone is told "poor you" beyond the point of being shown polite concern, can that someone truly be expected to rise from the crisis and fight like a wildcat? Not on your life.

People who are pitied to the point of *overconcern* rather than just *concern* often end up believing: *(a)* they have been treated unfairly, *(b)* they cannot survive the cruel blows of fate, and *(c)* they should feel immensely justified in getting depressed over it.

So much for the other person's suffering. What about that of the other-pitier? Can it even begin to be proved that anguish, tears, and heartbreak are of any assistance to the other sufferer? It cannot. When the other-pitier suffers over the misery of another, it's simple arithmetic: addition, not subtraction.

Isn't it bad enough that he or she is going through this suffering without another person also joining in? If we already have suffering in the world, do we need more? One neurotic at a time is enough, isn't it? The other-pitier thinks not, joins the neurotic sufferer and adds to the total misery in the world rather than subtracts from it.

2. Concern, not overconcern, is the moral stance that can be taken by the nonvictim.

To some extent we are our brother's keepers or we would all be hermits. To care for, to want to help, to identify with another person in distress is a mark of civilization. To disregard another human's suffering (or even an animal's for that matter) is to return to the jungle. The happy medium lies, therefore, between caring too much (overconcern) and not caring enough (indifference). And how is the sensitive and caring person to know when care is overdone? When has that invisible boundary between concern and overconcern been crossed? Simple! When it hurts.

Concerned surgeons do not go into a depression as they cut away at their patients. The agony, the expense, the disability the patient may suffer are not unknown to the physicians. Yet they do not respond with neurotic overconcern, because it would seriously interfere with the operation.

Instead, caring surgeons keep their feelings down to a sane level where they can still function (concern) without letting the experience get to them deeply (overconcern).

3. To pity someone overlooks completely an extremely therapeutic issue: *it could be worse.* (Solzhenitsyn, 1975)

If you but look about, even casually, it will become abundantly clear that millions of people are worse off than you. Are you blind in one eye? Many are blind in both. So don't be ungrateful. Are you paralyzed on the left side? You could have been paralyzed on the right side also. Were you demoted? Millions have never even had the job you had. Be grateful! Did your parent die? Millions have lost their entire families in accidents or war.

No matter how bad life gets for you, never forget that it could be worse. It is this philosophy which gives victims of the Russian prison system the ability to endure unbelievable hardships. Solzhenitsyn (1975) assures us that suicides and mental breakdowns are much lower than one would expect from such a population. Why? Because these inmates have learned to be thankful for every bit of good fortune they have. And to each misfortune they respond, "It could be worse." And that attitude saves their sanity and their lives.

ANGER

1. With two exceptions, all anger is neurotic. (Hauck, 1974)

Anger is the emotion you give yourself because of someone else's misconduct. Surely that's foolish. Why would any logical persons deliberately hurt themselves *after* someone else hurt them? That is double jeopardy. Instead, if you were to avoid anger when an injustice was committed against you, the total sum of anger is nil. Otherwise your happy frame of mind is lost, your appetite is disturbed, your blood pressure rises, and in some cases your very life is threatened when you allow yourself to get mad. So, no matter how you look at it, anger is self-defeating (neurotic) in most circumstances.

One exception is the use of anger to protect your life. You may do a better job of fighting if you first make yourself hopping mad. Under the pressure of an emergency frail persons have been known to excite themselves to such a degree that they have been able to lift heavy weights from pinned victims, or to trounce several attackers at the same time.

The second exception against the rule that all anger is neurotic is mock anger. There are many instances when the *pretense* of anger gets results which are needed quickly and harmlessly. The mother who scolds her son for running into the street may actually not be angry at all, because she knows all children will try to leave their yards and wander out into the neighborhood. She knows also that she could talk to him nicely to warn him of the danger. However, to assure herself that he will not run into the street again, she wisely *pretends* she'll wring his neck if she ever catches him doing that again.

2. Anger is an act of grandiosity, no matter what the cause. (Ellis and Harper, 1961)

When you boil it all down, your anger is a demand that you get your way and that the one you are angry at does not. That's it pure and simple. Now, how can you logically insist *you* must have your way and thoughts but others cannot? Why, because you're right? Nonsense. All anger is righteous or you wouldn't get angry. If you have righteous anger, then so does your opponent. Anger means to be righteous, so don't refer to your righteous position as though you had something unique. You don't.

Anger is a temper tantrum in the adult no less than it is in the child. The only difference between the adult's anger and the child's is the goal. The child wants an ice-cream cone, the adult wants a promotion. The child wants to stay up to watch television, the adult wants to sleep late Sunday morning. Aside from the goals, the principles are precisely the same. Your act of anger says straightforwardly that you not only want something but *because* you want it, you must have it *regardless* of what anyone else thinks. How grandiose can you get?

Suppose someone thought you were a fool and you became angry believing no one has the right to have such thoughts. Wouldn't you be acting like God? Wouldn't you be saying that no one can have thoughts you disapprove of? How would you like someone controlling your thoughts? Would you mind it if your skull were opened and parts of your gray matter scooped out so that you wouldn't have disapproved thoughts? Figuratively that's what you do when you get angry if someone crosses you.

3. Anger usually leads to two neurotic responses: more anger in the attacker and fear in the victim.

That's not very healthy: we get either a potential bully or a potential coward for our efforts. The bully becomes more angry if he sees fear developing in the victim because he knows he can lord it over the scared person. And the more angry he becomes, the more fearful the victim feels. A neurotic cycle of anger, fear, anger, fear is set in motion which can have serious consequences for both.

4. People have the right to be wrong.

This is just about the most difficult argument for a great many people to accept. Nevertheless, we are all imperfect, in as many ways as there are people. This simple fact gives us every right to be wrong. We have the right to think that two plus two is five or that the earth is flat. Others have the right to think we're stupid, or lazy, or to take advantage of us. That doesn't make them right of course, but then they don't have to be.

If someone has the neurotic right to distress us, then don't we have the same right? Of course we do. We can be as screwy as we like. It's our right. Then why don't we? Because it hurts. The abrasive persons we become because we give vent to our anger make us unliked and lonely. Bloody noses and frequent arguments are our inheritance for being mean. If we don't mind, we continue. If we do mind, we deny ourselves our right to be inconsiderate and live more happily.

5. There are no bad people in the world, there is only bad behavior. (Ellis and Gullo, 1971)

This is a particularly difficult idea for people to accept. All of us have been raised with the belief that there are good people and bad people and that the latter are by nature worthless and mean. Some are thought to be "bad seeds" or to inherit evil qualities from their parents.

Granted there is a whole lot of objectionable behavior in this world, ranging anywhere from telling a white lie to genocide. People who believe they have a right to judge others as bad because they behave badly fail to consider that at least three excellent reasons exist for this unacceptable behavior.

For instance, because people are imperfect they often blunder because they are deficient (they lack certain skills and abilities); are ignorant (they have not had the opportunity to learn certain behaviors); or are disturbed (they cannot conform to proper conduct even though they have the ability and have been taught to do so). If these inhibiting conditions can be prevented or removed, the person's behavior will conform to more acceptable standards.

A second argument takes the view that to judge a person by his or her behavior is logically insupportable. Persons and their actions are never the same, and if we are to be rational beings, we had better deal with them separately.

Judging a person by his or her actions is invalid because (Hauck, 1976):

a. Making a judgment of a person based on *one* trait is clearly not an adequate representation of that person. People are complex and possess many traits, characteristics, and talents.

b. However, we cannot make a judgment based on many traits either because no one has scientifically proved how many traits would adequately represent a person. Could it be two traits or two dozen, or two hundred?

c. Not only do we not know how many traits it would take to describe a person, we also have no idea of exactly which traits to consider. Each person would have his or her own list.

d. Assuming such a list were possible, would each trait be weighted equally with every other trait? Or would some traits, such as honesty, be more descriptive of a person's character than a trait such as punctuality? Such weightings have not thus far been offered to us.

e. Assuming further that a list of traits with agreed-upon weights might be devised, who is to determine those weights: you or I, or the citizens of Chicago, or all the members of the American Association of University Professors? No arrangement could be agreed upon to the satisfaction of everyone.

f. In the remote event that all the former objections could be removed there still remains a last and crucial objection: traits are in a constant state of flux. Today we are more honest than we were yesterday. But tomorrow we will be less honest than we are today. This being the case it is quite apparent that we cannot make judgments about people based on their traits if those traits are always changing.

6. Severe punishment or blame does not generally correct misbehavior, but if they do, the by-products of such correction often give rise to new misconduct.

Curse a boy for being a fool and he soon learns to put himself down so convincingly that he acts like a double fool in short order. Or torture a man for a crime and he is either spooked into a depressive-anxiety state for the rest of his life, or he is turned into a vengeance-seeking machine who will create a great deal more havoc before he must forcibly be stilled.

Firmness with kindness, not kindness alone, seems to be the best combination to bring about lasting and healthy change. This can sanely be expressed with the use of such healthy emotions as irritation or annoyance. On a continuum of least to greatest anger these milder emotions can energize people into productive action while not encouraging difficult side-effects.

JEALOUSY

1. A jealous person has the mentality of a slave driver. (Bychowski, 1968)

A jealous man believes he owns his lover body and soul. Therefore, he denies her the right to dance, speak, kiss, telephone, or look at another male. If that isn't slavery, what is? So, if a woman doesn't want to be someone's slave, she mustn't let *his* jealousy control her life. This problem is his. He should take care of it. He can get counseling and learn how to control his jealousy. Why should the woman turn herself inside out over his problems? He's saying it's her responsibility to stop him from being jealous. She mustn't believe it. It's his responsibility.

2. The problem of the jealous person is not distrust of the mate, but distrust of oneself.

If you don't think much of yourself, you're also going to believe you're not worth much either. And you certainly aren't going to think you'll have much holding power over your lover. If a man talks to her, you'll immediately think you don't have enough appeal to win out over the other person. In other words, you won't *trust yourself* to beat out your competition. You'll believe every Tom, Dick, and Harry can snatch away your little cream puff because every man in the whole world is superior to you. In short, the jealous person suffers from a massive inferiority complex.

3. It is pointless for the jealous person to insist the lover "tell the truth." (Hauck, 1977, 1979)

The only answer a jealous person will accept to the question, "Have you been unfaithful?" is a "Yes" response. A woman can tell her husband "No" a thousand times and his doubts will not be laid to rest. Nothing she can say can assuage his neurotic conviction that he is a totally unlovable jerk. But, if she says, "Yes, I hate you," or "Yes, I love someone else," he'd believe *that* statement instantly.

The upshot of the matter is this: if the jealous person isn't going to believe any statement but one that admits guilt, if he is *that* certain he's right, why ask? He apparently knows the truth before he inquires. Debate is superfluous. For this reason I advise all victims of jealous inquisitors to resist answering dead-end questions. No matter how much pressure you get to explain why you are three minutes late I urge you people to throw the responsibility for the jealous person's distress back to him where it belongs and to insist you will not respond since it does no good, and if he is still jealous, tell him to go to a counselor and have the problem taken care of.

WORRY AND FEAR

1. Catastrophizing is the cause of most emotional disturbances. (Ellis, 1966)

Stop and think about it: if you never believed anything was horrendous, could you *ever* be upset? How? Albert Ellis made a profound statement when he said that catastrophizing is the first step toward almost all other forms of emotional disturbance.

I see the process as follows: You make mountains out of molehills and this results in a generalized feeling of distress. You then proceed to give this indistinct emotion specific form, one of four forms, it seems to me. And these forms can exist almost simultaneously since they can express themselves one after the other in swift succession.

The four derivative forms this distress can take are: depression and its companions (guilt and inferiority); anger (expressed at times as hate, resentment, or bitterness); fear (sometimes seen as worry, anxiety, phobias, or panic); and poor self-discipline (procrastination and escapism).

If you did not believe in the first instance that some event was horrible, terrible, unbearable or calamitous, you could not get depressed, angry, afraid, or hesitant about facing your problem.

2. Very few events are truly catastrophic. (Ellis, 1962, 1966)

All of us have reacted to thousands of situations as though they were the end of the world. Not getting the raise you expected was perceived by you equally as tragic as an atomic war. You can only get just so disturbed over anything (short of psychosis) and you have often done precisely that, treated a triviality as though it were a tragedy.

Dropping out of school, getting pregnant at sixteen, breaking up a love affair, or being sent off to war are usually reacted to as though these are totally unbearable experiences. But these events have been endured by literally millions of people who later led happy and productive lives. What was thought to be a tragedy in reality was only a matter of regret, inconvenience, discomfort, or sadness.

The point is made by some RET practitioners that nothing is catastrophic, except by definition. That may be too far-fetched for many to accept. Nevertheless the point can still be made that the vast majority of frustrations only *seem* at first blush to be devastating when in fact they are tolerable and even growth-producing.

3. Focusing obsessively on a problem often increases it. (Fischer, 1970)

Worriers are horrified at the thought that life will become unbearable if they do not focus on their crisis. They believe the only reason they have not been overwhelmed is that they treat the matter very seriously, not casually. To urge them to put aside the problem scares them.

Worrying about a disaster can more easily make it occur. If you focus on the possibility of having an auto accident, your thoughts will not be on driving, they will be distracted from the traffic and be focused on an accident. What better way to induce a collision? The more you worry about something the more likely it is to occur. It is much better to do what you can about an issue and then get it off your mind and try to enjoy life. This includes such worries as losing control, having future anxiety attacks, harming someone, or having lewd or evil thoughts. All are *more* likely to happen if concentrated on obsessively.

4. To overcome a fear, face the fear gradually. (Marx, 1970)

No increment, no matter how small, is insignificant if it gets you closer to overcoming your fear. The the young boy who fears school is well advised to go to each class and bear it as long as possible before giving in to the urge to escape. If he cannot do that, he can at least walk into the classroom, sit at his desk, pretend to be looking for something, and then leave. Is this too fear-provoking? Very well, advise him to go to the door of each classroom and step over the threshold and then leave. And if that is too much, have him walk past the door of each classroom. Should this exercise induce panic, have him walk around the school from the outside. And if that is too much, have him go by the school each day, getting closer and closer to the front steps until he can finally enter the main door, go down the corridors, and into his room.

Such increments, especially when they deal with social situations, are not to be ignored. The client often does, but the counselor knows better and therefore gives praises for the fine effort. The adolescent who fears rejection from girls does not need to go up to a girl and ask for a date before we praise him for courage. We do the same even if he makes a phone call, hangs up the phone before she can answer, only touches the phone, even just *looks* at the phone, or only *thinks* of looking at the phone. Progress is the accumulation of steps toward the goal in the same way that a million dollars is possible through the amassing of pennies.

Going faster than this snail's pace is of course allowable only if it does not panic the student. It is this eventuality which had better be avoided lest your client experience a serious setback, in which case he would need to be brought back small steps at a time anyway.

5. Feeling fear is neurotic. (Mahoney and Thoresen, 1974)

The client who insists it is only natural to fear flying for the first time, or speaking to an audience of hundreds, or picking up poisonous snakes is quite right. It is a common emotional response. However, to intimate that it is also reasonable and healthy to show such fears, I believe, is mistaken.

To perceive a situation as physically, socially, financially, or psychologically harmful is one thing. To conclude that you have no recourse but to *feel* fear over such possibilities is another. The issue is over whether you will be only *concerned,* rather than *overconcerned.*

For instance, if you believe that the plane is unsafe, or that accepting an offer to speak before hundreds on a subject you are uncomfortable with, or that you will die if you touch a rattlesnake, then simply don't do it. But if, for some reason, you were required to perform these acts you could do each without feeling afraid even though you might be harmed. You would take your chances that the plane flight would be safe, that your audience wouldn't stone you on the stage, and that you might grab the rattler behind the head and avoid its bite. Each has its risk. The consequences could be serious.

These possibilities, however, don't make you afraid. Otherwise, to be consistent, you would shake every time you stepped into your car, heard an airplane overhead, or slept in a home with a gas furnace. You could be maimed or killed every bit as easily from those as the former. Yet, are you likely not to drive a car because it could crash and burst into flames? No? Then how do you justify not flying on the grounds that a plane can crash and burst into flames?

See the irrationality now? That's neurotic thinking pure and simple. You can know that something is dangerous and then avoid it or go with it and not be upset greatly in either case. Feeling fear means you have correctly concluded that an activity may be dangerous *and* that you *must* become disturbed over it, that you *must* focus on the possible pain at all times. Doing that causes you to die a thousand times without even being scratched. You anticipate harm but usually do not get hurt. Everyone has faced injury thousands of times more often than actual injury has occurred.

Such behavior is neurotic because you are giving yourself suffering (fear, anxiety, worry, or panic) over the possibility of future suffering. That's like committing suicide because you know someday you'll die.

Being concerned over future pain (cautious) is rational and healthy. Being overconcerned (fearful) is unhealthy and can be reduced if not eliminated.

But what if you were diagnosed as having terminal cancer? Would it still be neurotic to become afraid? Of course it would. Bad enough to die before your time without also going out of your mind. If you're going to die of cancer in three days, have a ball, not a nervous breakdown.

Furthermore, such self-control is possible and has often been demonstrated. Some Christians trembled as they were pushed into the Coliseum's arena full of lions. Others sang hymns of joy that they would that day be with God in heaven.

Sir Francis Drake put down a mutiny aboard his ship and arrested the ringleader (Durant and Durant, 1963). He offered to put the man in chains, take him back to England for a trial, and expected to see him hang. Or he offered to take him ashore at the nearest island, give him a last feast, and then behead him.

The mutineer calmly chose the latter. Later that day the band of men ate and drank merrily and told of memories they had mutually enjoyed. When it was time to get on with the execution the mutineer quietly apologized for having a short neck but hoped it would cause the executioner no difficulty. And he was beheaded without whimper, tears, pleading, or struggle. He went out in remarkably good spirits apparently (considering the situation).

6. Fearful acts can be performed in a state of fear. (Hauck, 1975)

When dealing with fears one is likely to assume it will be possible to face fears someday *when* one learns how to calm down. Any homework assignments such a person gets are usually delayed because of the conviction that one simply cannot be expected to perform fearful acts while one is afraid. This person, therefore, will not climb mountains, talk to strangers, give public addresses, and so on, until he or she feels far less afraid than at present.

The counselor is advised to make the point strongly that this is totally irrational thinking. To get over one's fears, one has to face the fears regardless of whether one is afraid or not. It is by doing the thing that one is afraid to do that makes the fear disappear. Therefore, advise your client to give speeches despite the fear. Climb mountains *because* of the fear. Speak to strangers even though to do so is uncomfortable. To do otherwise is to put the cart before the horse. One wants to be calm first and then do the fearful things. Reality dictates do the thing one is afraid of first, despite the fact that one is afraid.

Fear does not prevent anyone from doing anything. It provides persons with a rationalization. In truth, performing an act while afraid is a great deal more difficult than when not afraid. But it is still possible. Soldiers leave their foxholes under conditions of severe fear. But they do it. Stage performers have for hundreds of years been nervous and performed anyway.

To overcome a fear, a three-step process is called for: *(a)* don't blow the problem out of proportion, *(b)* don't think about it all the time, and *(c)* don't expect a fear to go away until you face it. That means to face it *while frightened.* In this way you can learn that your fear is irrational because you'll probably survive, not die as you thought.

7. Avoiding a problem *can* be healthy. (Watson and Tharp, 1972)

We are always told to face our fears, not to avoid them, and that it is unwise to run away from our problems. Sound as this may be, there are exceptions to this rule. When you have done all you can about your problem, you have not escaped or avoided it, have sought help for it, made preparations for whatever consequences might follow, then it is perfectly sound to get the problem out of your mind. The less you think about it, the less disturbed you will be by it. You can do this by distraction or simply by suppression. If you distract yourself, you will become busy with all kinds of pleasant activities and pretend the problem did not exist. This is tension-reducing.

It can even be carried to the point where you may ask the members of your family not to bring up the conflictual subject. A pending lawsuit, for example, once turned over to a competent attorney, and which may be dangling over the family's head for months, had simply best be dismissed from table discussion. The less people talk about it, the less they will think about it, and the less they will be disturbed over it. When you cannot do anything about something unpleasant, do not dwell on it, do not even mention it. Isn't this very much like putting your head in the sand? It certainly is. And I recommend it highly. Why get bothered by something you can no longer do anything about? Discourage table talk about it unless someone can come up with a pertinent way of dealing with the issue that has not been discussed before. In this way the involved persons can live through numerous unpleasant experiences without obsessively focusing on the serious consequences of their problems.

8. People who worry about pain and unhappiness are champions at tolerating pain. (Hauck, 1975)

It is ironic that the man who worries so much about the pain he may get if he develops cancer makes such a nervous wreck out of himself that he has nothing but pain from that day forward. Those persons who ruminate about how awful life will be if their parents would die suffer endless moments of anxiety for months or years in anticipation of that event. When a woman tells you that she would not be able to endure a certain frustration, reassure her that she has already endured more by worrying about that frustration than she ever would if that frustration happened. Has she not already lost sleep? Has she not had moments of great tension and fear? Would it not be easier in the long run literally to suffer the thing feared and be done with it? No matter how much the client argues that she cannot help getting nervous and upset over some anticipated pain, it can always be pointed out that the greatest pain has already been endured by the obsessive anticipation of it.

PROCRASTINATION

1. Delaying dealing with difficult tasks is usually foolish and eventually costly or painful. (Robins, 1966)

Sometimes problems go away if we ignore them, but not often. Reality clearly tells us that avoiding hard decisions, playing when work beckons, not putting away for a rainy day, all hurt us in the long run.

Difficult tasks are like weeds. They grow taller, the roots go deeper, and they spread out to ever and ever wider areas if they are not attacked when detected.

The young man who does not graduate usually pays for his inferior education for the rest of his life. The shy girl who will not introduce herself to her fellow workers during the lunch hour eats alone. The housewife who believes she will not throw a good party avoids learning from her mistakes. And in addition, she will not be invited to other homes if she does not reciprocate.

The poorly self-disciplined man believes that he cannot stand frustration and that any immediate action which removes that frustration for the moment should be taken. He journeys through life in a quest for one quick pleasure followed by another. He should be the happiest of men. How untrue! This poor deluded fellow who is forever chasing the rainbow winds up deeply frustrated, unfulfilled, lacking self-confidence, and fearful of life. He is the picture of unhappiness.

2. Procrastination is justified in two instances. (Hauck, 1976)

If you know you have a terminal illness or you are going before the firing squad at dawn, why discipline yourself? For what reason should you not eat, drink, sleep, and travel to your heart's content? Not to live to the fullest when you are fairly certain life will be brief is folly.

It also makes sense to relax from time to time merely to have relief from your usual life of strict self-discipline. Isn't life to be enjoyed? To take a break from your jogging or dieting makes it easier to return to those routines when you do not allow them to be compulsions. This does not work well with behaviors that are likely to become fixated, such as smoking, drinking, or using addictive drugs. Total abstinence is usually the best choice of action for these conditions.

LOW SELF-CONFIDENCE

1. Self-confidence is the result of three processes: *(a)* daring to do something, *(b)* analyzing your errors, *(c)* trying again in the light of what you have learned.

It is not enough to be risk-taking, although that is immensely important. Merely doing the same thing over and over is no guarantee that your performance will improve. Practice does not make perfect. You may be practicing your mistake and reinforcing it and thus getting worse over a span of time.

To improve with practice you must examine, analyze, and debate with yourself as to what you are doing wrong. Don't waste valuable time and effort hating yourself for your mistakes. Profit from them. Study them. Find out in detail how you went awry. Armed with this new knowledge, try a second time. And examine your performance a second time and then try a third time, and so on.

2. People have the perfect right to congratulate themselves after making a mistake and *knowing how to change it.* (Watson and Tharp, 1972)

Instead of downing yourself as millions of neurotics do, appreciate fully what has happened. You tried something, you found out you were wrong, and now you know what *not* to do next time. Eureka! You have learned something. Isn't that important? Isn't it the product of some daring, some effort, and a drive to learn?

So why do you punish yourself when you have benefited so much? Be glad you have the openness to realize you erred because then you can change. If you were so defensive that you didn't let yourself know you erred, you'd repeat that act endlessly.

Therein is the paradox. No matter how often you make mistakes you are not "failing." As long as you are trying (discovering new errors) you are not failing. Failure is doing nothing.

PERFECTIONISM

1. Compulsively striving for perfection is neurotic. (Hall and Lindzey, 1970)

It's one thing to want to be perfect, and another to make it a condition of your worthwhileness. Those persons who demand perfection of themselves get away from being tense and afraid of failure only if they have the talent of a Beethoven or a Picasso. The rest of us (being lesser mortals) approach perfection with greater struggle.

Instead of putting such an impossible burden on your back, why not accept the idea that doing is more important than doing well? By not caring mightily about your performances you tend to be more relaxed, to enjoy your task more, and to be less afraid of finishing what you started.

Perfectionists are often tense, worried, and ready to feel enormous guilt over an inferior performance. Therefore they fear completing it lest they fall short of their neurotic goals. And they are steadily in doubt about their work and are enjoying it little because they surely know they are not geniuses. The upshot is that perfectionists achieve near-perfection at great cost to themselves, or achieve far less than those persons who only *want* perfection.

The notion that winning isn't everything, it's the only thing, fails to qualify unless an unusually high standard is justified. For instance, if your life depended on winning, you might have a point insisting you had to win. Short of that, however, it is not necessary to win, only highly desirable.

The quotations we all learned as children, "If you can't do it right, don't do it at all" or "If it's worth doing, it's worth doing well" are in part nonsense. How do the proponents of this absurd philosophy expect persons to get good at anything if they aren't allowed to do badly at first and for a long time thereafter? Did they ever see a child get up from the cradle and run a marathon? Did they ever see a painter dash off a masterpiece the first time he picked up a brush? Of course not. Skills come with much trial and error. And anyone learning a skill had better count on doing it poorly for a long time before appreciable gains are noted.

Perfectionists are humiliated with trial and error. So they avoid trials, avoid errors, and avoid distant success.

SELF-ASSERTION

1. People do not need to be taught to *be* assertive, only *when* to be assertive. (Hauck, 1979)

Standing up for your rights is ultimately a matter of self-preservation. As such it is a practice engaged in by most people when seriously threatened. It is not a question of whether you would tell your boss to drop dead if he ridiculed you in front of your co-workers, it is only a matter of *how much* abuse you will tolerate before you do so. If you don't stand up for yourself when the boss insults you, perhaps you'll attack when he pushes you out of the way. And if that isn't enough, perhaps you'll act when he accuses you of stealing materials from the factory. A point comes when almost every slave, every coward, rises and rebels against tyranny. The same applies to the shy, the passive, and the accommodating. They too will spit at the boot that kicks them when their patience has run its course.

Cowards have, therefore, no cause to rationalize their fear. They can and will turn into bears when they decide they've had enough. Rather than spend a lifetime under the yoke they might just as well assert themselves now since *they will do it someday anyway.*

2. The price of assertion is, first, considerable unpleasantness and, only later, satisfaction. (Hauck, 1979)

Getting your way is seldom accomplished without risk or suffering. Growing up is painful and if you haven't the stomach for it, you remain under the control of others—also a painful choice. There's the rub. Break the grip on your freedom and you face certain resistance. Accept the grip on your freedom and it leaves you even more hurt. Those persons who expect their independence without a struggle are going to be sadly disappointed. One person in a thousand accepts a request to change with grace or ease. Most persons put up a whale of a battle upon being asked or forced to modify their behavior. This is in accord with human nature, like it or not. What you consider just is easily considered unjust by the person who is expected to change.

When a mother is fed up with her daughter's impertinences and grounds her for coming in late, the expected response will be a worsening of the relationship. After an assertive act things get worse before they get better. It's human nature. The only times this is not true is when the person being asked to change is so understanding and mature that the justice in the request is acknowledged at once. The fact that the relationship deteriorates at the outset is not proof that the assertive act was a serious mistake or that the plaintiff had better back off. Growth and change are sometimes not possible without struggle and suffering.

Persons who go on strike, declare a cold war, or stand up for their rights if they are tired of having their life run by someone else may not get the love they want, but they will earn respect. And from this the love may grow. Without it love is not likely to arise or to endure.

3. People have an obligation to themselves *and* to others to be *reasonably* self-centered. (Hauck, 1977)

Persons who seldom look out for their welfare are like those who seldom bathe: they are offensive to themselves and to others. What is as pitiful as a doormat disguised as a human being? As a gutless wonder you present a threat to all who depend on you. Finally, what will others think of how you are shamelessly ignoring your own welfare?

Even more serious is the tendency for the aggressor (whom you do not resist) to become increasingly more dictatorial. Is not every bully the product of a vacuum left by lack of courage? How can the aggressor get a foothold if at every turn the bid to do so is blocked? Slave drivers are impotent if people refuse to become slaves. The weak, the Pollyanna-ish, and the fearful are the creators of their own nightmares. Turning the other cheek when dealing with power-hungry neurotics gets the other cheek slapped as well.

INFERIORITY AND CONCEIT

1. Persons are never categorically inferior or superior to anyone else. (Ellis, 1973)

You cannot be inferior to anyone unless you specify the particular skill, trait, or action in which you are comparing yourself. Being a poor athlete means you can't throw a football as well as others on the field can. That's almost all it means. You can't conclude you're an idiot, a gangster, a poor tenor, or a worthless person from the fact that you play ball poorly.

The same applies to a positive action. Being a star quarterback means you play great ball and that's all. You are not a superior jogger, boy scout, chef, or person because you are a superior passer. One has almost nothing to do with the first three and nothing at all to do with the fourth. A person's acts and the person are not alike. There are no inferior or superior people in the world, just people who are strong or weak in certain ways. Never judge people by their actions, just judge their actions.

If you do this for yourself, you not only will never suffer from self-blame, guilt, inferiority, and the depression that goes with them, but you will never suffer from conceit either.

Being good at something and knowing it and saying so is not a statement of conceit. It is a statement of fact. To be conceited, you would have to add the thought that you are better in *all* ways, to others, that you are superior as a person because you are superior in a particular trait.

It matters not which trait you may praise yourself for. You can insist you are brilliant, gorgeous, sexy, creative, or generous. These are traits which describe performance, an infinitesimal part of you. They don't make you better than others who are tender, mature, or witty.

BRAINWASHING

1. Accusations are not automatically believed because they are repeated endlessly. (Ellis and Gullo, 1971)

You may have made the assertion yourself that you couldn't help believing that you were dull because your sibling told you so a thousand times. It is still not true. Wives who have been accused for years that they were selfish, and husbands who were accused for years that they were unfaithful, and who insist they were brainwashed, are mistaken.

An accusation is believed because you fail to analyze it carefully. It doesn't matter that the accusation was made once or a thousand times. If you believed it, maybe it's because you didn't think about it.

The teenage girl who takes her mother literally when told she's a slut for coming in at one A.M. isn't thinking. Suppose her mother told her she was a parking meter. Would the girl believe her? But would she believe her mother if that remark were made ten times a day for ten years? Of course not. Why? Because the girl would compare her mother's accusations with reality.

Is she a parking meter? Well, is she? Does she stand up all day and night? Is she made of metal? Do people drop coins in her and then turn a knob on her body?

Because of this analysis the girl could in no way ever be

brainwashed into believing she was a parking meter, or a door, or a horse, or a slut.

The next time your client insists, "It must be so. I've been told it thousands of times," disagree. It can't be so. Your client let it happen.

Chapter 5

Marriage Counseling

Emotional disturbances do not usually occur in vacuums, i.e., independent of interpersonal involvement. Some problems, such as self-discipline, are *intra*personal in nature. These are in the minority. The troubles and disturbances a counselor is likely to encounter often involve parents in conflict with children, workers in conflict with employers, women in conflict with neighbors. The most frequent conflict among adults, however, is between husband and wife. The counselor who does any counseling at all will certainly be called upon to assist in these difficulties. Rather than seeing each person individually, the counselor may want to take advantage of the benefits of seeing both parties together. At least six reasons can be cited for justifying counseling couples over counseling individuals.

REASONS FOR COUPLES COUNSELING

1. It is timesaving. Just as it is usually not much more difficult to teach ten children than it is to teach one, so it is often as easy to counsel a couple as it is an individual. While one is being addressed, the other is listening and learning, and probably applying what is being said.

For the couple who is experiencing similar emotional difficulties marriage counseling is ideal. If both are losing sleep and worrying over a financial crisis, the lessons on how to cope with fear are applicable to both. If husband and wife find themselves in an endless round of nagging and faultfinding, the techniques for controlling anger and resentment are as appropriate to the one as to the other. The counselor can focus on theory, then use examples from their lives to clarify the theory, and repeat this as often as necessary until the desired effects are achieved. This will make wise use of the joint session and satisfy their need for individual attention as well. While the one mate's problems are being looked at, the other will be gaining the same understanding with possibly greater compassion as a bonus.

2. Another advantage of joint counseling is its ability to provide a live demonstration of the couple's interaction. The evidence is immediately present, not subject to memory distortion, and therefore undeniable.

One gentleman who insisted he was not the faultfinder proclaimed by his wife had his perception of himself drastically altered during one session in which I interrupted the conversation between them each time he was critical of her.

"There you go again, Mr. Pick. Notice that you just compared your wife unfavorably to your mother?"

"I wasn't being critical of her, doctor. I merely wanted to make a true statement. After all, can't she listen to the truth once in a while?" was his equally bitter reply.

Again the living proof was gently placed before him. "Now you're telling her she can't face the truth. Isn't that another fault we have to add to the list you've already made in the last half hour?"

Back he came with more. "What have I done? I'm trying to tell you what she's like and now she's turned you against me. She's always doing that too."

"Just a minute, Mr. Pick. There's no need to get upset. I'm not blaming you. I am trying to show you an unpleasant habit which you don't realize you have. You *are* critical of your wife. That's been amply demonstrated, I think. Why, in the last few breaths you've told her she was inferior to your mother, that she childishly hides from the truth, and that she makes others disrespect you. How can you ever expect to get on good terms with your wife if you treat her that way?"

In this manner the counselor, by using the client's immediate behavior as another live demonstration, showed this highly defensive male what he was doing and encouraged him to examine his actions and beliefs. Here, too, it was the added advantage of couples therapy over individual sessions which presented the problem so effectively.

3. Perhaps the strongest reason for couples counseling is the restraint it places on the parties. Couples seldom talk over their difficulties at home in the same relaxed manner they assume in a professional's office. At home they tend to be extremely impolite, to rehash their past misdeeds, and to inflict as much new injury as possible. If these attitudes begin to arise in counseling, they can usually be effectively thwarted by the intervention of the counselor. His very presence as an outsider dampens their overt hostile expressions, and he can step in when the talk becomes meaningless or spiteful. He can always show them both how they are creating their own emotional misery, thereby indirectly encouraging further expressions of wrath.

If his presence fails to have this quieting effect, he may find it wise to see them separately.

4. Couples counseling is clearly indicated when the problem involved is not necessarily between the parties but with a third person or a frustration they hold in common. A difficult child, an interfering relative, or a mutual inability to make friends, for example, would all be sound criteria for seeing these two persons together.

5. When the degree of disturbance is approximately equal between the mates, joint sessions can be quite profitable. In this case, neither partner will feel singled out as being at fault and the other totally wise. Then, too, the amount of involvement for each is likely to be balanced, thereby avoiding one client getting all the attention while the other becomes bored.

6. If the couple asks to be seen together, this can be honored. A spirit of cooperation may underlie their antagonism and express itself in this form of wanting to work out their difficulties side by side with all cards on the table. The oppo-

site may also be the cause for this request. One partner may be suspicious and distrustful of all that would transpire in individual sessions. Together each knows all that the other is saying. If it later appears to be an unwise decision, the reasons for recommending individual sessions can be discussed.

REASONS AGAINST COUPLES COUNSELING

1. If one or both partners are likely to spend their hour discharging emotional tensions at each other, they had better be seen separately. Such time is too unproductive to overcome the many advantages from couples counseling. Such therapy quickly becomes a dreaded event which would lead to premature termination. Persons who exhibit such meager self-control are further hurt by joint sessions because their memories are refreshed over past indignities as each tells one side of the story. One party may also feel embarrassment by having faults paraded "unfairly" before a person whose approval usually means a great deal. Though these explosive episodes can be turned to good advantage by demonstrating accurately how the couples interact, they serve no good purpose if occurring frequently or intensively.

A not uncommon complication is the expectation on the part of the injured mate for the counselor to take sides against the attacker. Disillusionment follows refusal.

2. Some problems are so personal that good taste commands privacy. A couple may appear to have a mutual problem when in reality their difficulties really stem from a third but unspoken reason. A man may be under constant criticism from his wife because of a recent increase in his drinking yet she be unaware that he was having an affair. Obviously marriage counseling might not provide the opportunity for this secret to be expressed at that time.

Or if a problem were fully known, but of a highly delicate nature, separation could be considered. A man accused of rape will hardly want to discuss this problem before his wife no matter how helpful, forgiving, or sharing she wants to be.

As always, let good taste be your guide.

3. Some souls are so sensitive about their personality makeup they do not relish the thought of being exposed to anyone, not even the professional. We might look to the I.Q. as an example. I am convinced many adults are extremely curious about how high their intelligence is but will not ask for an intelligence test because the psychologist would share this intimate knowledge. If a reliable, valid, but self-administered I.Q. test were available, I am certain it would prove to be a highly salable item.

The same can be said for a man's inferiority feelings. He may know only too well he has them but would be loathe to admit it to others or to discuss them before his spouse. For this reason a couple that otherwise might qualify for marriage counseling will ask for separate sessions. As long as such sensitivity is present this request for privacy could be granted. It often happens during the course of individual counseling that such areas are mastered and the suggestion for joint interviews then can be made by the counselor with some assurance of acceptance.

4. Not the least of reasons for separating a couple for counseling is conversation domination. Though one spouse may accurately relate some of the problems between both, the laconic partner's personal needs are not likely to get the attention they deserve. Some clients play a subordinate verbal role in the presence of the spouse but are perfectly capable of clear, forceful expression in the absence of that person. When it appears to the counselor that one mate is not joining into the discussion actively enough separate sessions can be considered. The change in communication which emerges is sometimes startling.

DIPLOMACY IN MARRIAGE COUNSELING

In marriage counseling it is absolutely essential that the counselor be on guard against showing repeated favoritism. This does not mean you cannot agree with one and show up the errors of the other. This you can do if you are ever to be of service, since it lies at the heart of RET counseling. What you want to be cautious of, however, is responding emotionally so that it appears you and one of the mates have taken sides. The counselor who frowns at the wife after her husband reports she has brutally beaten her child will achieve nothing but the loss of her goodwill. The therapist could more diplomatically respond in this fashion: "I am very sorry to hear that, Mrs. Carver. This must be very distressing to you. However, there has to be a good reason for your behavior. Why not tell me about what happened and perhaps I can help you avoid losing control again in the future."

Additional comments could ask her not to blame herself and explain to the husband also why his wife is not to be reprimanded harshly even though she is responsible for a grave misdeed. In this way the counselor will not alienate the husband because his complaint is not ignored while the wife can feel she has a sympathetic ear to speak to.

If the couple offers conflicting versions of a problem, the counselor can once again sidestep accepting one as true and the other as false lest the injured party henceforth feel misunderstood. If Mrs. Carver protests her husband's statement by declaring: "It's not true that I beat Cindy, doctor. Sure, I spank her when she's naughty, but to listen to John one would think I abuse the child every time I lay a hand on her," the counselor can then decide which of his clients is the more stable. He then addresses the less stable spouse, momentarily agreeing with him or her and asks why, if this is correct, the partner has not been able to be persuaded.

"There seems to be a disagreement here, Mrs. Carver. Suppose we go along with you and agree that your husband simply fails to see that you're not being unreasonable in your discipline. I wonder why you've been unable to convince him you're right and why you upset yourself so much when he accuses you falsely."

This line of investigation will, in all likelihood, bring forth numerous other complaints and irrational ideas which can serve as valuable insights for the counselor in gaining a more comprehensive understanding of their dynamic interplay.

More importantly, for the moment he has avoided the trap of taking sides and acting as judge.

Underlying all such therapeutic strategies, whether performed deftly or not, must be the heartfelt conviction by the counselor that neither party is truly blameworthy, only ignorant. This may involve ignorance of the seriousness of the behavior (the mother may really not have realized she was damaging her child) or ignorance of knowing how to control her rage. If she adopts this accepting attitude, it will be difficult for him to play favorites regardless of his lack of technique.

Sad to say, there will be occasions when all persuasion fails and the counselor must take a stand. A Mrs. Marvel spoke stingingly about her husband's custom of dancing with other women at his company's social events. Rather than immediately insist she was being neurotically narrow-minded, I tried to show her there are better ways to encourage him to dance with her. She could, for example, learn to be a much better dancer. With enough lessons she might even be the envy of the party and be in great demand by other men. Perhaps his envy might be heightened thereby and urge him to seek her out more constantly. She could be further advised to be more loving and pleasant when rejected so that he might feel so warmly toward her that he would gladly forgo the pleasure of dancing with others. These maneuvers might make her realize how her behavior was creating *less* desire in him to give her the complete attention she demanded.

When these suggestions brought no results it was decided to confront her with a direct disagreement that her husband was really in the wrong. She was told that his divided attention was not an impoliteness on his part but a failure on her part to regard herself as worthwhile. She apparently had no confidence to mingle with others and give the impression to other men that she would not enjoy being asked to dance. If she tried and was not invited to dance, her fear of being undesirable would be common knowledge.

Her husband joined in with a sarcastic, "See, what did I tell you?" type of remark. To avoid the charge of favoritism the husband was told: "Wait a minute, Mr. Marvel. Why are you getting angry with her? Just because the two of us disagree with her we need not suppose she will automatically change her mind. I'm sure she still believes she's right. And why shouldn't she? She has every right in the world to think as she pleases, even if we think she's wrong. Right now you are telling yourself she can't disagree with you and that's nonsense. She never has to change her mind, even if she does so out of spite."

In this way the counselor achieved two valuable goals: he demonstrated his goodwill toward the person he disagreed with, and he showed the mate how to accept that person despite the disagreement.

THE RECIPROCITY THEORY OF LOVE

Love is that powerful feeling you have for someone who *will* satisfy, who *is* satisfying, or who *has* satisfied your deepest desires and needs.

That is why you love your frustrating children—as annoying and as unfulfilling as they may be for months or years. You still love them in anticipation of the day your children and you can have a more satisfying relationship.

You love your aging and senile parents for all the kindnesses they have performed for you in the past even though they can no longer serve you.

My definition of love doesn't sound like anything new, does it? Let's study it closely and you may get a surprise.

I claim you love people only *after* they have pleased you. Love is the outgrowth of getting your way so completely that you would find it almost irresistible to ignore your benefactor. It is a *conditional* thing: satisfy my deep desires and needs and I'll love you; don't satisfy them and I'll fall out of love. The notion that you will love your sugarplum "till the end of time" is sophomoric. It all depends on how long and completely she can satisfy your desires and needs.

Consider the following observations: If you wanted a beautiful, witty, and wealthy woman for a wife, you'd love her *only* as long as she were beautiful, witty, and wealthy. If she aged ungracefully, lost her wit to depression, and made unwise investments which caused her to sell her Mercedes, your love would gradually dissolve as surely as her appeal.

If during the ten years you two were married you discovered a number of other ways she was able to make you happy, you might not want to fall out of love because those new benefits would outweigh the lost ones. Instead of being witty she might have become intensely curious and stimulating. Her beauty might not be regarded so highly by you ten years later because you have grown and don't judge flesh above character as you did as a younger man. Her loss of wealth might not distress you either because you might have become independently wealthy and wouldn't need her funds any longer.

My theory also answers those persons who are unhappy because they are not being loved "for themselves." They object that their mates constantly want them to change, as though that were unfair.

From my definition of love you can see that you don't love the person (as desirable as that would be), *you love what that person can do for you.* If that person does a load of nice and important things for you, your love increases. Otherwise it declines. That's why love is often an up-and-down thing. From period to period you are largely getting or not getting most of what you want from your mate.

This theory of love also throws light on two conditions usually not taken seriously as love: love at first sight and adolescent infatuation.

Love at first sight is certainly not like a love developed over a fifty-year struggle. If that is your criterion, then love at first sight is nonexistent. However, if love is the feeling you have for someone who will, is, or has satisfied your deepest desires and needs, then it is valid to call an overnight romance a real love experience. The lover is taking enormous risks, of course, when he gives his heart to a girl whom he sees across the crowded room on some enchanted evening. He is basing his feelings on a few clues which are skimpy and immature in nature. She moves well, has a lovely laugh, long wavy hair, etc. He knows nothing about her health, her thinking habits, her moral values, and so on. If he did, he might quickly dump her and realize she can in no way satisfy his desires and needs.

If love is as I say it is, then it is possible to love more than one person at the same time. Why should it not be possible for two or more men or women to satisfy you? If you had the time and energy and could get around enough, it's perfectly feasible to be truly and deeply in love with half a dozen potential mates simultaneously.

THE BUSINESS THEORY OF MARRIAGE

Marriage is a loving business. That's the title of the book I wrote in 1977. I made the claim that marriage is an agreement between two persons who decide to have a partnership in almost the same way two business persons enter into a partnership.

John, for example, decided to settle down, to have companionship, safe and convenient sex, and to raise a family. So he looked about and met Mary, who also wanted those goals. Sensing this mutual satisfaction of desires and needs, they married. But along with those common goals there were a number of other spoken and unspoken aims each of them had which will direct the course of the marriage. The more they each understood exactly what the other wanted the better chance there was to make each other happy.

So John selected Mary and expected her to make breakfast in the morning, to stay home to raise the children, to have sex every Friday night, and to spend Christmas in Florida. Mary has her own priorities. It is hoped that they do not differ significantly or the marriage is not likely to survive.

John could be said to have hired his wife to perform certain services, and Mary hired her husband to perform services important to her. To make the business work, each will have to put pressure on the other if one is falling down on the job. No need to ask, "Do I have the right to expect

John to help with the wash?" If Mary hired him with the expectation of getting help with the laundry, then that's one of the requirements for the job of being her mate. And if John doesn't fulfill her job specifications, she should do the same to him, her employee, that she would do for any other employee.

First, Mary would talk to him nicely and let John know that she was frustrated by his behavior. If he didn't change, she'd call him on the carpet again and make the point stronger. Eventually (to make a story short) she'd fire him. That's exactly what he would do with his secretary, or janitor, or gardener. In business it's called firing. In marriage it's called divorce.

As an employer you have the right to expect anything reasonable from your employee. If the latter doesn't like it, he can petition his boss, but if that doesn't work he can quit. And the same is ultimately true of all married couples.

DETERMINING THE DEEPEST DESIRES AND NEEDS

A marriage is a harmonious arrangement only as long as each party receives a *reasonable* degree of contentment. When two persons come for counseling it can usually be assumed that one or both parties were frustrated over not having his or her deepest desires and needs satisfied. As a counselor you can immediately assist them by finding out what those frustrations are, and find them out in detail. After listening for a while to their complaints, I usually arrive at a point when I want to find out which frustrations will have to be removed to restore harmony.

I ask one of the couple: "What must your mate do to make you happy? What do you want so that you will feel loving again?" Then I list the points each party makes.

This is an extremely important step. Without it we simply don't know how to proceed. How can love be restored if they do not have a clear idea of what efforts need to be made to please their mates? It is at this point that the counselor asks them to make three determinations:

1. Are these frustrations clearly *understood?*

Simply because she says she wants more love from her husband doesn't mean for a moment he truly understands her. When she says she wants more love and affection is she suggesting that she wants more sex, more companionship, more freedom, more money, or to have her back scratched?

Frustrations are not clearly understood by vague statements such as, "Be nice to me," "I want more freedom," or "Don't boss me." What do they mean? Niceness, freedom, and bossiness are vague terms. They mean one thing to the wife and another to the husband. The counselor therefore queries each to learn what he or she thinks the other wants.

One client wants his wife to lose weight. But how much? Five pounds? Ten pounds? He doesn't know? Then what does he mean? Further query reveals that he wants her to get her weight down to the point where she can wear a bikini. Ah, now she has a clearer idea of the task that lies ahead.

After it is clear that the *conditions* for love are understood, proceed to the next.

2. Are the parties *able* to remove the disappointments for each other?

The lady in the above example, now that she knows precisely what her husband wants of her, asks herself if she can in fact lose the weight. Does she have the self-discipline? Would it embarrass her to wear a revealing swimsuit? Would her friends laugh at her for not acting her age?

Or, is this request easily met? If so, we proceed to the third question.

3. Are the parties *willing* to satisfy the deepest desires and needs of each other?

Just because your client *understands* what the mate expects, and is *able* to meet those requirements, doesn't mean he or she *wants* to meet them. If your client can and wants to gratify the frustrated partner, the frustrations will diminish and the feelings of love increase in direct proportion to the degree of satisfaction. Well and good. You hope that married couples can usually work out their problems in that neat way.

When one or both partners cannot or will not meet each other's deep desires and needs three options are open to them.

THE THREE OPTIONS

For the sake of clarity let me list the choices a partner has when not getting the changes desired.

OPTION NO. 1: Give In. Don't make waves. Tolerate your state. You may correctly think that the issue is not big enough to bother with, certainly not to get a divorce over. Life with your mate isn't *that* bad and if you don't get what you want in this respect, well, it's not the end of the world. Besides, you've tried getting tough and it hasn't worked, so it's time to realize your mate can't or won't change.

OPTION NO. 2: Protest. Assuming that the usually benign methods have failed to get your mate to please you more and that sweet talk and greater kindness will not work in the future, you can take Option No. 2 and go on *strike* or declare a *cold war.* You can take the position that your mate will have to be forced to change, that the frustrations you've been living with cannot be tolerated, that you are being quite fair to expect a change and that no matter how upset your mate gets the change is still essential. You (the husband) cannot tolerate a sloppy house or carelessly prepared meals. You (the wife) do not want to tolerate your husband's chasing every skirt in sight. The wife can stop being a neurotic perfectionist, and the husband had better stop spending money as though it was going out of style.

Persons who choose Option No. 2 tend to be assertive and to feel there is still great merit in their marriage. They want to fight for their marriage rather than leave it, and they have faith in their ability to withstand the pressures they are about to create.

When you go on strike you declare war. A deliberate crisis

is invented with the full expectation that you will irritate, hassle, annoy, anger, and frustrate your mate to the point where he or she realizes just how determined you are to get a change. It's a tricky game to play because things get really bad before they get better, *if* they get better at all. It's a gamble, but one worth taking because the stakes are so high.

If you go this route, be prepared for a deteriorating relationship. Stay with it until you get the concessions you want, or until you can't stand the flack. And be sure to reward your mate for every concession.

OPTION NO. 3: Separation or Divorce. If all else fails after pressuring your mate, you may want to avail yourself of Option No. 3. Your attitude then is: "I've had it. I choose not to live like this any longer. I think I may have some feelings for my mate but they're irrelevant. I don't want to live this unhappy way another day."

THE TEST OF COMPATIBILITY

Keep the definition of love in mind and the meaning of compatibility becomes immediately clear. *When you enjoy pleasing each other you are compatible.* If it upsets you to make your mate happy, you're not compatible. It's that simple. If you have to give, give, give to make your mate love you, forget it. You're not compatible. If it takes being miserable to make your partner happy, why do it for long?

You did not enter into marriage to please your mate. You did it to please yourself, first and foremost. It was a self-interested move. To make your partner happy with no consideration of how that effort affects you is foolish. The person who thinks a marriage works best when the mate is repeatedly satisfied is going to find out eventually how miserable life can get.

Compatibility results from a reasonable *exchange* of favors, not a unilateral give-and-take. One of the quickest ways to ruin a marriage, a friendship, or a working relationship is to give to the other person with no thought of reciprocity.

You cannot be compatible with a person who resents pleasing you.

It is your responsibility to get enough satisfaction from your partner so that you get your deepest desires and needs fulfilled. If you don't, it won't be possible to love that person. And your indifference is often a direct result of your not pressuring your lover to make you happy. Therefore, to protect your marriage you had better pester your mate until you feel so satisfied that you feel happy. How happy? To the point where you can say you're *just reasonably content* (Hauck, 1979).

THE JRC

To make any relationship satisfying you need to fight for enough benefits until you can say: "Now I'm just reasonably content. I could stand to have my way a great deal more. But, if I didn't get any more benefits than I'm getting now, I could stand this relationship."

Look at it this way. Suppose it takes 2,000 calories a day to keep you physically fit. If you take in 2,100 calories every day, you gradually gain weight. If you take in only 1,900 calories every day, you lose weight. If that 1,900-calorie diet continues for weeks or months, you can get to the point where you're a skeleton.

The JRC is analogous to the 2,000 calories. Suppose it takes ten strokes a day to keep you just reasonably content. Ideally you'd like fifty strokes a day but are content with ten.

Now let's say you get only nine strokes a day. If that goes on for months or years, and you don't use RET on yourself constantly, the day can come when you're so emotionally and psychologically starved that symptoms show.

Recently I counseled five persons who lived chronically below the JRC. They followed the predictable pattern of many persons who go through this process: (1) they dislike themselves for being so cowardly that they permit others to abuse them; (2) they dislike the person doing the manipulating and abusing; and (3) lastly they hate the relationship. Then they want a divorce.

Had they made their mates uncomfortable enough to *make them* sacrifice some of their desires and needs and have been content to a reasonable degree, these three forms of disturbance would not have occurred.

To live chronically below the JRC usually takes its toll. *If you don't know how to dismiss frustrations gracefully, you're going to pay the price with symptoms of disturbance.* You may twitch, become insomniac, be depressed, or bite your nails.

The five persons I mentioned above had the following consequences from allowing themselves to live below the JRC for extended periods. One started stuttering after four years of living with a cold and indifferent wife. Another was taken advantage of shamelessly for two years until she actually had murderous fantasies. A third was so lonely she over-ate to tranquilize her nerves. The fourth had an affair she would not give up even though she felt intensely guilty over it. And the fifth, a fellow whose wife put him on the bottom of the totem pole to her folks and the children, suffered a major depression.

THE USUAL SEQUENCE
IN COUNSELING MARITAL PROBLEMS

A theory is all well and good, but if you can't apply it to your work, who needs it? Study the theory on the previous pages and then apply it loosely in the following sequence.

A couple comes to you with the complaint that the woman is depressed because he leaves her alone too much.

1. Proceed to discover how serious things are. Has she seen an attorney? How long has she felt neglected? Was she ever depressed over this matter before? Was she counseled for it? Or hospitalized for it?

You might learn that she has made this complaint off and on for the past four years. She is ready to see an attorney if marriage counseling doesn't bring some relief. Thus far she has not needed hospitalizations or medications for the depressions because she worked them through by herself.

2. Allow the second party to express his views. Does he agree that he leaves her alone too much? He doesn't? Then what is her problem in his opinion? If he agrees, find out what he has done and will do about her frustrations.

These two steps need take no more than fifteen minutes, ideally. Now that you have your bearings you will want to formulate a program they can follow and provide a rationale for why it could work.

3. List what each now expects from the marriage. Since she is the plaintiff ask her first, "What do you want from your husband that will make you love him deeply again?" Then make a list of from one to a half dozen desires she enumerates. Don't allow him to interrupt at this point to defend himself. Just get the facts first.

Then get his list of expectations. Make sure they are as precisely spelled out as is reasonable. If he says he wants more freedom, find out what that means. Does he want to be gone four nights a week? Until midnight? Doing whatever he likes? Or does he mean a poker game Friday nights until eleven P.M.?

4. Explain to them what love is and how a marriage works to bring happiness. Point out that they are in trouble because one or both are not having their deepest desires and needs met. This automatically causes them to love each other less. And because they each entered into marriage with the hope of having their desires satisfied, the marriage can survive happily only if they achieve Options No. 1 or 2.

She, for example, has the choice of not making so much of her frustration and learning to dismiss it gracefully. Does she want to do that? No? She has been doing that for the past four years.

Very well, then, she can decide to go on strike and make him so miserable with her pressures and lack of cooperation that he might give in. "But he'll get angry," she protests. No matter. The time for more talk is past. She had better act if she wants results. She is encouraged to get enough satisfactions until she can truly say: "That's more like it. I can live

this way even though there's a lot more I'd like to have."
That's reaching the JRC. It is pointed out to her that it is her
responsibility to get the benefits from the marriage that
would make her happy. She is miserable now and the marriage is in danger now, because she *allowed* him to get his
way so much that there was nothing for her. I tell her that
she's 50 percent responsible for this state of affairs even
though she thought of him for years as the sole culprit of her
unhappiness.

If the husband interjects that he's not going to tolerate her
assertive actions because she's not right, or because it would
be unfair, support his stand. Tell him that he too has a right
to his deepest desires and needs and that if he is unhappy he
had better take Option No. 1: tolerate the conditions she is
putting forth; or Option No. 2: go on strike and be prepared
for a cold war until it gets so bad he can't tolerate it any
longer, or until she gives in, or until a workable compromise
has been reached; or Option No. 3: separation or divorce.
He's fed up, doesn't want to try any longer and now is quite
content to get out completely.

5. Advise them to go home, think over their options and
have a long talk over a cup of coffee. Also, set up another
appointment for each separately if they hinted at wanting to
talk to you alone, or if you think one party needs further
understanding or encouragement. Otherwise have them back
as a couple.

6. Clarify last-minute objections. The defendant (the husband in this case) may protest strongly that he is being asked
to make all the concessions.

Don't dispute this. Merely point out again that the reality
of his situation is this, like it or not, fair or not: his wife is
very unhappy and falling out of love. If he wants to remedy
that, he had better satisfy her deepest desires and needs or
she'll end up: *(a)* more depressed, *(b)* angrier with him and
considerably less loving, *(c)* increasingly indifferent about the
marriage itself.

If he wants the marriage to succeed, he had better listen
to her and make her happier even if he loses somewhat in the

process. Urge him to give until it hurts *and then to stop.* There is no point in his becoming miserable to make her happy. That's turning tables on each other and is no improvement over what they are already going through.

What if he does give until he reaches his JRC and she still isn't happy? What then? Then he has the same three options to choose from: *(a)* convince himself that not getting what he wants isn't all *that* bad, *(b)* pressure her to accept some of his terms, or *(c)* leave her.

Experience in counseling couples is essential in applying this formulation. Once you try it a few months and have my views of love and marriage clearly understood, you'll be surprised and pleased at how you can bring order out of chaos for two persons struggling with their love lives.

MARRIAGE COUNSELING WITH ONE PARTNER

The contention that marriage counseling is not only best when both parties are involved but essential is overstating a good point. I see no reason why a single member of a marriage cannot get help for both.

For example, if one feels quite abused and unappreciated, assertion training for the passive member makes perfectly good sense. In most cases the party at home, after he or she begins to feel the pressure brought on by counseling, is only too eager to have a chance to influence the counselor.

Aside from that, the man or woman who comes to you can be made to understand the dynamics of love and marriage without the other present. The marriage has every chance of improving if the client can be taught individually to tolerate the other's behavior or to pressure the mate into a reasonable change. The mate is unnecessary to the process even though his or her presence is desirable.

I want to dispel the notion that we must always observe the complex interactions between man and wife. When they come for counseling the delicate negotiating has obviously not worked. The feelings of the partners are so bruised that major efforts, not minor ones, will be required to bring a resolution to their differences. That means decisions will be made which are egocentric in nature. They involve mainly his welfare, or her welfare, first and foremost. That's what the problem has become. The aggrieved member of the marriage has failed to make it selfishly satisfying. To correct that error requires counseling *that* person to be more self-centered, a task that can obviously be done in individual therapy.

TAKING SIDES

I don't tell either partner which of the three options he or she should take. That's up to them. They will live with their decision a long time, and if things don't work out to their satisfaction, I surely don't want to be held responsible.

In other matters I freely take a stand. If the husband thinks he has the right to go to a bar alone but his wife does not because she's a woman and could get picked up, I do not hesitate to back up her protests that he's being unfair.

When the wife insists he has no right to go out by himself I disagree and support his right to make himself happy. If she doesn't like what he does to be content, she can learn to accept it (Option No. 1), bother him to change (Option No. 2), or leave him (Option No. 3). And even though I may not approve of his actions, I can still take sides and support his right to be wrong.

You won't lose your client if you are not personal in your disagreements. Be objective, try to understand why someone chooses to behave a certain way, and your comment may not sound like criticism as much as advice.

KEEP AN OPEN MIND

A client can come to you with stories about his or her mate that can turn you against the absent partner with considerable intensity.

Be careful. You're hearing the opinion of only one person, a very prejudiced person besides. Even if the statements made against the mate seem perfectly consistent and reasonable, keep an open mind and a closed mouth. You do *not* know the other person. So don't make judgments.

Then what are you supposed to do until and *if* you get a chance to see the other person? You won't be much help to your client if you hold him off until you can see the wife too. So I usually say something like: *"Assuming* what you've been telling me is accurate, then I have the following observation to make. But don't go home to your wife and say, 'Dr. Hauck said this or that.' My comments are colored completely by *your* view of things. If I had a chance to talk to your wife, I might get an entirely different opinion of what's wrong between you two."

I assure you, taking this advice will save you a great deal of backpedaling during your counseling career.

CRISIS THERAPY

Option No. 2 states that your couple may iron out their problems with a *confrontation* of their respective desires and needs. This is advised only when more pleasant and civil methods have repeatedly failed. The second option fosters pressuring a mate continually and in increasing degrees until one or the other budges, or until there is an acceptable compromise, or until they separate or divorce.

Some couples may protest this scheme, thinking that greater love is not likely to emerge by such nasty tactics. And at the outset they are almost always right. Things almost always get worse before they get better if the clients pursue this program. However, things continue to worsen if they don't follow it. By creating a crisis deliberately there is at least a chance that irritation will bring a thoughtless mate back in line. Without confrontation the imbalance gets worse and worse until the abused partner creates the greatest crisis for a marriage: a sudden divorce.

Do not let your client rationalize out of creating a crisis for a change. Point out some of the following observations:

1. If you don't take a stand *now* against the unjust treatment in your marriage, you will take it *someday.* Why suffer

for months or years when you could face that issue now?

2. People do not listen through their ears as well as they listen through their eyes. It is what you *do* about a problem that creates movement, not what you *say* you will do.

3. When things get worse because you are creating a crisis it will seem as though all hell is breaking loose and your marriage is most certainly headed for it. Not so. In the vast majority of cases the exact opposite is true. When one mate gives endlessly and selflessly to the other mate without feeling just reasonably content in return, that marriage is in serious trouble because one party is falling out of love.

It is the duty of the frustrated mate, the one who is falling out of love, to fall back into love by seeing to it that his or her mate does nice things again. Only then will the sagging love feelings be strengthened. Note, however, it is not the contented mate who is expected to upset the applecart. It is the deprived partner whose responsibility it is to make waves until satisfactions are more evenly balanced.

When this is attempted, the marriage is put under its greatest strain. It is a make-or-break proposition in contrast to an avoidance and decaying situation. The person who is being pressured to change will rarely be so mature as to say: "Oh, I'm sorry. I didn't realize you were being ignored. Of course I'll give up my poker games."

In most instances he defends his past practices by insisting he has been quite reasonable. Furthermore, he usually intends to perpetuate the arrangement by retaliating against his mate for being so unfair. He wants her to return to the nice ways of the past. To accomplish this, he may use a whole series of strategies. First he will argue, then pout, then get angry. These not working, he may become physical and misbehave badly. Perhaps he will begin to drink, or come home late, threaten to have an affair, or get a divorce.

This becomes the tensest part of crisis therapy. Things can get seriously worse, almost to the point where the marriage is about to break. And your client will feel certain that all is lost. Yet you have the right to be truly comforting and report progress. That is precisely how many changes are brought about: by creating a crisis, by a direct, nonviolent, confrontation. You can assure your client that he or she is on target, that the therapy is progressing nicely, and that the worse it gets the sooner we'll all know if there is going to be change or a separation.

What? Those are the alternatives? Certainly. No one wants to undertake creating a crisis until milder methods have failed. But when they have failed, the marriage is headed for a breakup anyway. However, it will take a long time and be accompanied by much unhappiness. Better to bring the boil to a head and lance it.

Only the deepest sense of confidence in the wisdom of this program can cause your client to weather the marital storm. Watch out for endless excuses to back away from confrontation for the sake of brief relief. If your client simply will not continue the cold war, alert him to what may happen and then sit back. When the marriage becomes intolerable again the confrontations can be resumed. And again, as things deteriorate, remind your client that the situation is actually improving. The worse it gets the closer you are to a resolution of the conflict.

BUT DO I HAVE THE RIGHT?

This is a question you will surely hear more than once when you try to teach assertiveness to your abused client. Does he have the right to have his way, to be selfish, to pressure his loved one into a condition of considerable frustration and perhaps disturbance, all for *his* peace of mind?

You bet he does. The problem in these situations is that the client has not been self-caring enough. That's why the marriage is going sour. It can only move along as long as *both* are usually in a state of JRC (Just Reasonable Contentment). To achieve this, the frustrated partner needs to apply pressure until he feels just reasonably contented. Then, and *not until then,* it is wise of him to stop.

The question, "Do I have the right?" can be answered: "Yes, you have the right to look out for your health and

happiness. Even more, you have the *obligation* to care for
your welfare and happiness or neither of you will have happiness as a couple in the future."

NO SECRETS, PLEASE!

Keeping secrets for one mate against the other is like
lying. You find yourself covering up one fact, then another,
and soon you are tripping over yourself to avoid revealing
facts you're not sure you covered up. I find that almost 100
percent honesty is the best policy. Therefore, I often remind
my clients not to tell me facts that they don't want the mate
to know because I have a short memory and may cause
trouble due to my forgetfulness.

One way to avoid keeping secrets (aside from declaring it
as a policy) is to see the couple together. You can't be used
as a solo confidant when the three of you are engaged in a
conversation. And of course there's always the option of
trying to assure your client that it is better to be more honest
with one's mate.

About everything? No. I have found that some people are
unable to tolerate every truth and still function maturely. To
tell a woman whose marriage is finally working itself out after
months of therapy that her husband had an affair fifteen years
ago is borrowing trouble. What good will it do her to know
this if it is not likely to happen again and if it reawakens old
doubts? If she is a strong, understanding, and forgiving
woman, then perhaps such news does no lasting damage.
However, if she is in a fragile frame of mind and you judge
that no good can come from such a revelation, then let sleeping dogs lie.

In those cases when your client is certain you and his wife
are going to have secrets it's important to tell the wife of his
accusation and that you will not be guilty of it. Then reli-
giously tell him whatever she conveys to you of a secretive
nature. It'll eventually get back to him anyway. You don't
want to be caught holding a confidence when you promised
you'd be open.

WHEN ONE PARTY DOMINATES

In the final analysis many marriages are bankrupt because one of the parties involved has been dominated and has his or her deepest desires and needs unsatisfied. Recently I talked to a woman who married when she was seventeen and has been dominated by her husband ever since. She is now in her thirties and is experiencing an unhappy marriage because every time she wants to grow and assert herself he puts her down like a disapproving father. As a dutiful daughter, she crawls back into her shell. In my further discussions with her I will use the father-daughter analogy because it describes very accurately what is going on. Whenever she allows herself to be dominated by her husband I can always compare her behavior to that of a little girl who is afraid of having Daddy angry with her. This is a piece of transactional analysis that we can well use.

The mother-son combination occurs frequently among alcoholics. These women wind up marrying weak husbands who lean on them and give the women a feeling of importance because the men are so desperate for help. However, like naughty boys who kick and fuss when they don't get their way, these alcoholic males threaten their wives with rejection and violence if they even entertain the idea of not being motherly and indulging.

In this case, too, I find it is helpful to use the mother-son relationship. I sometimes ask the woman if in the years of her marriage she didn't actually say to herself a number of times that she had another child. I am surprised at how often the wives have indeed said so and are surprised that I can put my finger on one of their private thoughts.

When talking to the husband I can use the same analogy, but I try to be careful not to use it as a put-down. He is not a fool because he depends upon his wife as a mother. I assure him that it is a human failing many suffer from but that nevertheless he would be wise to make every effort to change this tendency. Being a man, he will find it uncomfortable to think he is acting like a boy and perhaps will gradually make efforts to stop treating his wife like a mother.

A MARRIAGE SAVED BY OPTION NO. 2

This is the third session with this couple. They are both in their early twenties and both employed. At the first session Sue said that she did not love her husband any longer, that she was angry with him, and that their sex relationship was very poor. She indicated that she wanted to be more independent, to run around, to see things, and to not have to cook all the time. She felt that she had married too early and that she had missed a great deal. Although she felt that Arthur was the best husband any woman could ask for, she still complained that she felt she was living like a forty-year-old woman rather than a young wife who is supposed to be excited about life. Furthermore, it was her feeling that they were growing in different directions.

Arthur revealed that he wanted to have a better sex life, to have her help with the chores more frequently, and that she should be more predictable. Whatever pleasure she had only lasted for a short while and she would treat her belongings as though they were toys. She always wanted something bigger and better. In point of fact she did not know what she wanted.

During the first session I determined that they had very little idea as to what marriage was all about and had them read my book on marriage counseling. Then in the second interview, after one month's separation, they reported that things were moving along a little better because he had been more attentive to her and she forced herself to be more active by playing tennis and developing a social life which was somewhat separate from his. She was also hoping that Arthur would develop more ambition along the way.

This session clearly demonstrates how quickly crisis therapy can bring results and how neatly they progressed from confusion to harmony when they decided on Option No. 2: Protest. They broke their silence and talked honestly about their desires without guilt. Their one-month separation gave them time to learn what a divorce would be like and it pushed them into reconciliation. The cold war worked. It was a risk. But it was worth it.

This is the third session and they now report that things are getting better and they are considering terminating. This comes as somewhat of a surprise in view of the fact that they separated for approximately four weeks between the first and second sessions. The time involved from the first session to the present is approximately three months.

THERAPIST: How are things going now?

Art: A lot better. We do things. Yesterday we took a ride in the country and just looked around. We sat outside in the truck. We just sat there and talked and talked and walked around our place. I think we get along a lot better.

T: Can you tell me why? What are each of you doing to make things better?

Sue: It's like we've started all over from the beginning only instead of dating we're married.

T: In the beginning you said you wanted to get out. You were married too early and you wanted to have more freedom and so on. Now are you feeling this way again, Sue?

Sue: No.

T: Why not?

Sue: Well, I guess I learned to handle my—it's hard to explain, I wanted what other people had. They were playing tennis and things like that and they were going and having good times. I was around a lot of single girls and I wanted that because I was not happy at home. I was tired of being the housewife and working an eight-hour-a-day job and coming home while he was having a good time with his friends and I let all my friends go.

T: So what have you been doing since you have gotten into counseling?

Sue: I play tennis now. We play tennis together now once in a while. I just go more. There are times that I get out and go by myself instead of waiting for him.

T: Well, why didn't you do that before?

Sue: I had the wrong idea of what marriage was like.

T: What do you mean?

Sue: I thought that you had to be totally bound to each other. Just constantly always together, doing things, just the two of you together.

T: So since you have been satisfying some of your own desires more you're getting more happiness, you're getting more satisfaction from the marriage and you are not as resentful toward your husband?

Sue: I think we let our problem get to the point where we both ignored it to where it got out of hand. We just kept ignoring it. We wouldn't do anything about it. We never fought. We just let it ride.

Art: We needed somebody to open our eyes up to tell us what our problems were and so we could understand them I guess.

T: Well, what did I tell you that was helpful to you?

Art: I hardly had any feelings toward her. I just took her for granted. She took me for granted, I guess. Now we get out and do things. She comes out and helps me out a little bit. She stands there and talks to me. We can talk more.

T: In the process over our counseling have you been making your wife understand what it takes to make you happy? And, Sue, have you been doing this with Art?

(It is important that they understand why they are getting along better.)

Sue: We talk a lot more together. If something bothers me I don't like, I tell him and he tells me.

T: Why didn't you do that before?

Sue: I didn't want to make waves.

Art: I just didn't care. I just wanted to let everything slide and be forgotten.

T: You didn't want to upset the applecart.

Sue: Yes, instead of creating a big fight I just let it slide until we got to the point where I didn't care what he did and he didn't care what I did.

T: And you've been doing the opposite now. If you want

something, you let each other know. You talk about it. Is that what you are saying?

Sue: We talk more. We show more affection toward each other too. Instead of our sex life being an act, like you are obligated, it's not that anymore. It's what it should be.

Art: We were talking about it the other day and I told her it was definitely a lot better. I was a lot happier with her and with coming to you. I thought it just changed our whole life, turned it around.

T: Great. Tell me what do you think was the thing that turned this marriage around? I've only seen you people about two times before now and you've made some nice improvements. You've really changed. I can see this. I am trying to determine what you did that was so different. What did you learn from me?

(Do you see how difficult it can be to get people to examine their behaviors?)

Art: The biggest problem was me.

T: Can you explain that?

Art: I didn't do anything with her. I didn't talk with her. I went off with my friends. I rode motorcycles on Saturdays. I'd come home and hit the couch and fall asleep. She'd watch TV and knit, and do the dishes. She just got tired of it. I didn't talk to her hardly. I'd go drink beer with the guys after work on Friday nights and stuff like that. At one point in our marriage, when we first got married, I couldn't break away from my friends. I'd go out and drink beer and I came home one night at twelve o'clock at night. She'd get mad but she didn't want to say anything because we were just married. The next night I didn't come home until two o'clock.

T: Did you learn to register your protests more, Sue? Did you talk up more and not tolerate this behavior? Is that why you changed?

Sue: We understand now that marriage isn't all hunky-dory day after day. We understand that it is normal to fight and to disagree. Because no two people can agree on everything.

T: Okay, but you were fighting before.

Sue: Oh, when we lived in our apartment just after our wedding, that was for about a half a year. But when we bought our house we thought: Okay, this is it. We have a house, we're married, now let's fall into the pattern couples fall into. Everything is lovely, smile, smile. You go to work, you come home, you eat supper, you do what married people do. We got to the point where we were doing what people forty or fifty years old did—sit around and watch TV. There we were twenty years old. We had everything we could possibly want, but we just got to the point where in order not to make waves and make it look like everybody is happy we were fooling ourselves. To avoid an argument, we'd give in.

T: So then you simply covered over and didn't register your complaints and kept quiet rather than express yourself, and it's at that point where lots of things were happening that weren't making either one of you very happy. You were very unhappy with his behavior, but you didn't say anything about it. That's after you got into the house.

Sue: Well, he was still active, still going out and having a good time, and I was staying home being the little wife with the gingham apron and the skirt and the priscilla curtains, the whole works. That's what I thought it should be, that he should go to work and have no outside activities but come home.

T: Okay. Now since you've come to counseling you have done something different. Art has changed. Why? You're more satisfied. Why?

Sue: We came here because I thought that it was all me. I thought that I was bored. I didn't want to be married anymore, I wanted to go out and have a good time and run around. Now we've learned that the problem wasn't all me. It was partly my fault but Art will tell you that he thinks that he's the one that caused it because he got to the point where he ignored me. He didn't care what happened to me.

T: Why did you separate? Was that a suggestion I gave you?

Art: Yes.

Sue: Well, we asked you. We were going to separate, but we didn't know if it would hurt us more or help us more. We still had enough fight left in us when we came here and we wanted to make it work. We thought we'd just wait and ask you because you are a professional.

T: And I said, "Go ahead and separate for a while and see how things go."

Sue: And see if we needed each other.

Art: You said if that's what you want to do, maybe it's better to let her go and see if she likes it. Maybe she would come around in a couple of weeks and want to come back.

T: In the meantime, Art, while you were separated, apparently you discovered that you had a lot of feeling for her. You began to understand why she was unhappy and began to satisfy those desires with attentiveness, more company, and not taking her for granted. Then, Sue, you turned around and you felt more loving toward your husband because he was being more attentive. At the same time you also said, "Well, those times when I can't rely upon his company I'll simply go ahead and do something for myself so that I can get more kick out of life." So you took the bull by the horns and you did something for yourself.

Sue: Yes, for myself. I just thought, Well, I'm not going to sit around anymore. I got out and I entertained myself.

T: As I look over my notes you were saying, Sue, that you wanted to be more independent, to see more things and not just do cooking and housework. And, Art, you wanted more sex from your wife.

Art: I didn't just want sex, I wanted her companionship. I wanted her to come out and help me in the garage, talk to me, not really help me but talk to me, be there.

Sue: He wanted more from me, but he really didn't know how to ask for it. He just probably expected me to out-guess him.

T: Were you able to overcome that because you had some counseling? Did you see the importance and necessity of your expressing your desires?

Art: Absolutely. She asked me to take a day off work and spend some time together in the afternoon. I was working on the house gutters and she came out and talked while I hung the gutters and helped me out. She helped me hold the gutter while I cut it and stuff like that and we talked.

T: Is that something you would ordinarily have done or would you simply have said: "I don't want to ask her. I'm afraid to ask her. I'm too shy to ask her." Or what?

Art: I wouldn't have asked.

T: Why did you ask now? Somewhere along the line did I make it clear that it was important to express your desires and needs to the other person?

Sue: After we took those tests you gave us and you pointed out where our differences were, you told Art that he had to be more outgoing. I told him that a long time ago, but I guess it has to come from somebody outside for him to realize it.

T: Then, Art, you did force yourself to change in this respect?

Art: In the past if she'd come up to me and ask me, "Would you like to go play tennis?" I'd say, "No." But I went and played tennis and I loved it. I told her I'm ready to go again any time she feels like playing now. We feel we've worked out our differences nicely.

Sue: But, Art, that wasn't until after I decided to take Dr. Hauck's suggestion to separate for a while and then to take Option No. 2.

Art: Yes, I noticed that when you stopped all your yelling and decided to develop a social life of your own.

T: What did she do differently, Art?

Art: She told me she'd find other amusements if I didn't pay more attention to her. If I stayed out till two A.M., so would she. I didn't believe her at first, but the first time she didn't come home till late I decided she meant business.

Sue: That was the hardest thing I ever did. You once told us that backing up my convictions with actions was about the toughest thing I could ever do. You were so right.

T: You must have felt like you were taking a big risk.

Sue: I sure did. And once I saw how good I felt making my statement, I decided to do it several other times.

T: How did Art take that?

Art: I got mad.

Sue: He gave me a bad time, I can tell you. And I was ready to give in to him several times. It was only because I remembered what you said that things would get a lot worse before they'd get better that I stayed with my program. It was wonderful how confident I felt during this whole thing. I had a program, a road map so to speak, which I could follow during these episodes.

T: What did you remember?

Sue: That I should let Art have his way only if I could accept his conditions without being unhappy.

Art: She tried that too long. I learned real quick a few weeks ago she was through complaining and was going to do something instead.

Sue: That's when I decided to fight for my rights. I made waves and was determined not to back down until I got my way more.

T: Bravo for you. You apparently began to realize you had nothing to lose.

Sue: Sure, if I gave in to him, I'd be miserable and wouldn't stay with him, but if I stood up to him and he wouldn't give in, I'd lose him too. But I had a better chance going down fighting for my happiness than trying to make Art happy without caring much for my interests.

T: And, Art, how did you take this?

Art: I remembered what I read in your book *How to Stand Up for Yourself,* that people have an obligation to get enough benefits from their relationships to the point where they feel just reasonably content. I began to realize Sue was fighting for her JRC and I couldn't blame her. That's when I decided to give in more and see if I could make her happier.

T: Apparently you found out that you were also content to make her content—a most important discovery.

Art: Sure. When she asked me to play tennis and I tried it, I found out we could have an interest in common.

T: Well, I'm delighted that you are moving along this well. If at any point along the line things begin to go a little wrong, don't hesitate to come back and we'll give you a booster session or two and see if we can't straighten it out. Right?

Sue: I tell you this has been the best thing we could have done.

T: Thank you so much.

Chapter 6

Group
Counseling

Brief therapy is particularly well suited to groups. It provides an opportunity for instruction which is not possible to match with individual therapy. In group counseling you can actually give each member a chance to try out new skills in teaching others. Through such experience one learns to keep oneself stable.

My first step is to ask a client to present the problem. I may do the probing myself and treat the client as though we were in individual therapy, but it is done before the group. I gather my data, determine what the problem probably is, why the client is so upset over the problem, what he or she can do to gain relief, and prescribe homework.

The group, though not participating actively, can still be learning a great deal by listening and observing this interview. Thoughts will be expressed with which members can identify even though the problem under consideration may not be immediately relevant. People can learn a great deal merely from listening. Remember that a large part of RET is teaching.

I shall never forget an experience I had with a group of pregnant adolescents. One sixteen-year-old had great fear of pain. She even dreaded her weekly visit from her gynecologist at the maternity home where I was a consultant.

I didn't know she had this fear until after she delivered her child. She and I had never spoken of it. In a group therapy session of some fifteen to twenty girls I would routinely come around to her. But her self-consciousness prevented her from wanting to discuss her problem before her friends.

During the weekly sessions prior to her delivery I dealt with the problem of anxiety and fear a number of times in counseling with the other girls. I didn't know it at the time, but my quiet little friend was soaking up every word from those discussions. The net result was that she was learning in every sense of the word.

I came to the group one day and noticed she was absent. Her time had come. She went with a feeling of strength because she was now unafraid of the delivery process.

It turned out that she had a lengthy and painful breech delivery. Yet she took it without hysterics. No one would have guessed she had once had a neurotic fear of pain.

When I met her in the hallway two weeks later she confirmed the above account and added that she learned how to be unafraid by listening in group. She explained that she was certain she would have driven her nurses to distraction and been the terror of the maternity ward if she hadn't learned to control her fears of pain.

And I never talked to her directly about it, not once!

In a similar manner it is possible for every member of the group, whether feeling guilty or not, to benefit considerably from counseling a single person in regard to guilt. What one learns others can learn whether or not it is relevant at the moment.

The analogy of group counseling and teaching can be carried too far. Lengthy lecturing may have a legitimate place in the academic setting but rarely in counseling. One learns best who participates. Active learning is generally more efficient than passive learning. To get your students involved in the counseling process itself is just about the best way there is to teach RET.

To accomplish this, I conduct many of my groups as therapy practice sessions for the clients. I start with any client who is willing to tell us about a problem. The group is then asked to join in immediately and to continue the probing into the nature of the frustration. The group is urged to help the volunteer see how and why he or she is upset and what might be done to bring about relief. The group even winds up suggesting homework assignments.

As the session proceeds I interrupt when necessary. If the group is going astray, I bring it back on target. If the members want to deal only with solutions to problems, I remind them that problems do not cause disturbances. As sound as it may be to remove a stone from inside one's shoe, it is also sound to teach tolerance for such an irritation. Life does not always allow us the opportunity to permit its removal. Non-RET counselors tend to focus upon the reduction of frustration directly rather than upon the thinking behind the disturbance. So I break into their discussions and remind them to get deeper than events, to get to the cognitive structure of the disturbance.

In this way all the group members learn how to rid themselves of irrationalities. They are teaching each other under the watchful eye of the group leader. And as they learn how to detect and combat procrastination and emotional distress in one of their own, they are at the same time gaining control over their own habits.

The beauty of this method is that it makes group counseling an in vivo experience. The group's teacher, the group, as well as the single group volunteer are all being helped simultaneously.

If the group members are reluctant to play counselor, I explain the great benefits to be gained by trying their hand at teaching RET to someone else. They see this point quickly and lively sessions usually follow.

SIZE OF GROUP

A fetish has been made by many group therapists about sizes of groups. Some limit them to six or eight or even a dozen persons. For the experiential conditions they are trying to achieve, such group sizes are appropriate. These conditions are not likely to take place in very large groups.

Some subject matter is so sensitive (child abuse, incest, abortion, homosexuality) and some groups are so homogeneous that large numbers would make effective therapy ineffective or not feasible.

With these exceptions aside it is time we looked anew at the issue of group size. Look about you and see how people are being influenced. They're influenced in twos and threes, in families and gangs, and in groups as large as classrooms. So why not conduct groups for twenty-five? Or for two hundred and fifty? I have often lectured to crowds of two hundred and fifty. I've given seminars to over two hundred people. And if the response I received was sincere, I'd have to conclude that a lot of people got a lot of good by sitting in an audience for two hours once a week for four weeks and listening and asking questions.

"But that's not therapy," you protest. Yes it is. If people can learn about themselves in a one-to-one situation, why not in a one to ten, or twenty, or two million? Public television addressed to an audience of millions is daily instructing children and adults on a wealth of subjects.

"But that's not counseling," you insist.

Brief counseling with RET is instruction. It's instruction to one, or to thousands, or even to millions. Put me on television for one night for two hours and I'd ease more neurotic disturbances than a thousand therapists would accomplish working full time all their adult lives.

This means that group therapy can easily deal with fifteen or twenty, even twenty-five people, and still have enough intimacy to cope with most problems. That's the size of many classrooms. Again—what's the difference?

ADMISSION POLICY

Informality is the mood of my groups. I want to treat my clients as adults and therefore put the responsibility for their getting benefits from therapy on them. I'll do my share and am prepared to teach what I know. Whether they want to avail themselves of my knowledge is up to them.

This means I let them come and go when they wish. It's their money. That gives them the right to accept or reject my services just as I have the right to eat or not eat a meal I have ordered in a restaurant.

I get immediate feedback about how I'm doing by noting the attendance to my groups, the number of late arrivals, or even the number dozing. These are excellent indications of how I'm going over. I wouldn't want it any other way.

That's how I conducted my college classes. I never took attendance. I let the students come or go any time they wished as long as they were respectfully quiet and undisturbing of others.

I also put few conditions on the kinds of persons I would accept in my group. RET is so logical, so teachable, and so learnable that its appeal can extend over a range, from high to low I.Q.'s, from teenagers to senior citizens, and from passive to aggressive personalities. Who am I to say one can learn and another cannot? With the exception of the retarded, the severely disturbed, and the blatantly unruly, I allow all comers. I have been surprised more than once by how often a nondescript character from whom I expected very little became my star pupil.

EXPERIENTIAL EXERCISES

It is unfortunate that RET is so often identified by most counselors and the public alike as a method by which people develop a strong personality by being emotionally cold, rationally detached, and all in all not very likable. The specter of becoming a robot scares both professional and lay persons sufficiently that they shy away from the RET persuasion. Nothing could be farther from the truth.

RET counseling has no fear of dealing with things in an emotional way, at least if it is a pleasant and joyful emotion. We are opposed to institutionalizing or in other ways fostering the development of irrational emotions in dealing with life's frustrations. For this reason we advocate a great deal of reasoning in our therapeutic endeavors, but we certainly do not avoid experiential exercises either. There is no reason why role-playing, or empty-chair techniques and the like cannot be used in an RET group (Nardi, 1979). These methods quite realistically bring out feelings which people may very well be averse to showing. If it is important to get in touch with these feelings, whatever experiential process serves that end is appropriate. However, we believe that when a person confronts his or her negative feelings that the matter not be dropped at that point. Instead, we would definitely encourage a broader understanding of the issue involved.

For example, if one of the group is angry with an employer because of a bit of mistreatment and the leader finds it difficult to get that person to empathize with the employer, then an empty-chair exercise would not at all appear remiss. Or the member could take the role of the boss and thereby learn why the latter acted as he did. This is an effective method of getting some people to put themselves into another human being's shoes so they can appreciate the nature of the event from another perspective.

If the client now understands why the boss might have been unreasonable, the RET counselor is, of course, gratified but not satisfied. Not only in this particular situation, but in all situations the client needs to have greater appreciation for another human being's fallibilities. The client is then taught that there is no such thing as a bad human being because we are either deficient, ignorant, or disturbed. The basic principles of RET are again discussed and the particular irrational idea under which one labors is examined and the client is taught how to dispute it. When that is done, then not only is the subject freer from repeating that particular incident again, but is also freer from further hostilities in almost every other similar situation.

GROUP MEMBERS AS MODELS

It has long been recognized that one of the major advantages of conducting group counseling as contrasted to individual counseling is the ability of groups to provide immedi-

ate feedback to doubting clients. Those of faint heart and
little faith can often have their suspicions and incredulities
removed when they see what is happening to one of their
group members. For this reason it is important for the leader
to check up at each session as to how the various members
have fared since the last meeting. Once in a while a client
comes in who has done a fantastic job on homework and has
altered his or her life in significant ways. If one happens to
be outgoing and can tell a good tale besides, that might prove
to be most persuasive in getting others to see just how effective the counseling has been and how usable were the leader's
instruction and homework assignments. Perhaps it will dawn
on the remaining group members that if this one can make
such fantastic strides, then why can't each of them do the
same?

One of the ways to elicit such situations would be to ask
at the very start if anyone has some experience to report since
the last meeting. This can bring forth a number of reactions
that can provide the leader with an opportunity to correct
misconceptions, to clarify mistaken impressions, and to pick
out one person or several persons who have made advances
in their growth.

I try to examine in some detail just how an improvement
was made by encouraging the client to explain at leisure what
caused this growth and whether it coincided with my previous instruction.

Make sure that you compliment your star pupils for the
nice work they have done and assure them that they can
continue in the same vein if they apply themselves as they
have previously. But also direct such comments to the group
in general to assure the other members that they can make
significant changes beyond their expectations.

Modeling need not only be offered by clients but also by
the therapist as well. Probably with RET, more so than with
other methods, the clients are intensely curious to see
whether these fantastic statements which the counselor is
making can actually work, and especially whether they work
in the life of the counselor. To provide an in vivo experience

for them in the management of hostility or depression gives an invaluable demonstration of the veracity of the teachings. For the counselor to encounter a piece of bad news which they are all aware of and to handle it with dignity and calmness says more to them than seventeen lectures on depression. To be raked over the coals by an irate client and to respond with a calm assertive explanation is again far more convincing to a group than theoretical arguments. A counselor who is somewhat of a dingbat is going to have a hard time trying to show them how to conduct their lives in a sane way. Similarly if a counselor chain-smokes or is grossly overweight, it is difficult to appreciate his or her counsel on self-discipline. The more we can speak from experience, the more we are convinced of our therapeutic framework, and most importantly, the more we can *demonstrate* that it does work, even for us, the greater the impact will be on the ever-watching, observing client. Make no mistake of it, they are watching us like hawks trying to find out whether we are for real. The counselor who speaks with forked tongue and cannot live up to most of the high ideals others are exhorted to follow will have little credibility, and deservedly so.

Does this mean, therefore, that counselors must be infallible? Are we to believe that RET counselors must be above others in practically every respect and never show emotional disturbances of any kind? Of course not. We can have our grieving moments, our moments of procrastination, occasional angry flareups, and so on. But if we want to be taken seriously as professionals, we had better have significantly fewer of these episodes than the people we are trying to help.

USE OF THE BLACKBOARD

As counseling is frequently a didactic procedure, there is no reason why the group members cannot be treated as students. Try to acquaint them with the best literature which is appropriate for their separate problems. I ask them to read it before each session so that we might move along more speedily. First I check to see if the person is in fact the kind who likes to read and can benefit from reading. If I get a positive answer to both questions, I do not hesitate to recommend a bibliotherapy for those clients.

Another method that is certainly applicable to the situation is the use of the blackboard. This is didacticism at its finest. Practically all RET counselors have worked out diagrams by which they make theoretical points. It is frequently helpful to explain a point with which the group seems to have some difficulty. Through this visual medium I am often gratified by how clear an issue can become when it is sketched on the board.

Some people, however, are auditorily receptive while others are visually receptive. Some are doubtlessly proficient with both sensibilities. This is, therefore, another good reason why the use of chalk and blackboard is advised. Some people learn well by seeing while others learn well by hearing. Critical theoretical points can be explained nicely with letters, arrows, underlining, boxes, or what have you. List the ABC's of emotional disturbance, for example, or the three methods of becoming psychologically depressed, or the five reasons why people are afraid to assert themselves. Having these items on the blackboard provides the clients with ample opportunity to soak up what you are saying because they can look at it, see the words, see the sequence in which they are presented, and absorb this material much more at their leisure than is possible if only words are spoken.

From personal experiences I remember countless times when the group was not willing or able to accept RET thinking until it was diagramed. For many group members this was the technique that did the trick.

GANGING UP ON THE LEADER

Picture yourself as a counselor with a roomful of clients who have never been exposed to RET thinking. During the next hour and a half you will figuratively be telling these people such things as: two and two is five, the sun rises in the west, and Genghis Khan is the President of the United States.

Can you imagine what the reaction of the group would be if you literally tried to get such ideas across? They would gang up on you. They would think that you were off your rocker. Some of them would have a strong inclination to get up and walk out. Many of them would smile because they'd be certain you were joking.

Practicing RET asks that you present ideas to people which are almost as wild as the ones I just suggested. Yet, most people actually believe the outlandish things which we rational therapists want them to challenge. We do not ask them to believe that two and two are five, but we do ask them to think over whether or not they need love now that they are adults. We ask them to consider whether or not there are literally bad people in the world. We ask them to question seriously the idea that they and their behavior are the same. When we tell them they need never blame themselves for anything, it is like telling a group of patriots that the American flag is not red, white, and blue. Everyone in the group is going to gang up on you.

Make your statements as you need to, let them think you are crazy, then proceed to debate with them. If you know your discipline, you will have their admiration by the end of the session. It makes no difference whether it is one or two or a dozen who are challenging you. You will find that people practically always bring up the same objections. When you answer one objector, you usually respond to several others. Don't get nervous. Don't lose faith in your rational arguments. Always try to remember that these people are more disturbed than you are. You know something they do not know, and your role is to teach them what you have learned.

"What?" you say. "The counselor is different from the rest of us? Superior? Above us?" My answer to this is "Yes." I think it is time that we stop being humble about our superiority in matters in which we are supposed to be experts. Why am I leading a group if I am no better in these skills than they are? The only justification I have for taking their time and money to listen to me is that I have something to offer. I must know more about remaining emotionally calm than they do.

If I don't, then I have no business being in the position of a leader. So it is quite natural that I take a position of confidence *with respect to the psychological skills they want to learn.* No claim is made that the counselor is superior to these people in any general way, only superior as a student of RET and probably of other areas of psychology as well. I should not hesitate to admit that my accountant knows more about money matters than I do since that is his area of expertise. To do less is to profess false humility.

It is my deep hope that armed with these insights as counselors practicing RET when you find yourself the leader of a momentarily hostile group you will be able to clarify your points and win the group members over to your side. Don't back down. Stick to your guns. Lead them out of the darkness.

LOVE AND APPROVAL FROM THE LEADER

Positive regard for clients has long been thought of as an essential ingredient in the therapeutic process. Empirically it is easily established that when students like their teachers they learn better. When children feel loved by their parents they seem to turn out better also. When we converse with our clients, are on good terms with them, generally we get along better with them. To get on good terms, we solicit their friendship, are nice to them, show them that we care, and in the humane sense that we love them.

RET has no quarrel with the idea of our being decent to our clients. However, too often the point is made that the client is a worthwhile person because he or she is loved by other group members or by the leader. This can be a dangerous practice because it teaches clients that their self-worth rests upon the opinions of others. As true as it may be that the group and the leader have high personal regard for all of the group members, this does not reflect the world at large. When those people leave the group, sooner or later they are going to be rejected, put down, ignored, and abused. If they naively go through life insisting it is unbearable unless they are loved, they are going to have a difficult time of it.

I wish it were as some group therapists pretend it is. Life would be nice if everyone loved one another. The fact is there is a great deal of cruelty in the world and people are often petty and nasty. To carry on group work without somehow preparing people for these realities is an injustice to the group members who expect to function in an imperfect society.

For this reason as a group leader I never pretend to love all of the members in my group. I try to be decent and civil to all of them. But some I might not like particularly. I can accept the fact that they might not like me. And I try to teach them to accept that fact. I further point out that it is perfectly possible for them to learn whether I or others love them or not. It is perfectly possible for them to learn not to get depressed, angry, fearful, or to procrastinate even if they are not particularly fond of the teachers who are teaching these techniques. Stop and think about it yourself. Have you not had teachers in your life whom you did not especially like, but from whom you were able to learn a great deal nevertheless? It may well have been more pleasant if those teachers had treated you pleasantly. I don't quarrel with that. However, to suggest that learning is impossible unless the teacher is smiling all the time and ready to pat students on the head is simply unverified.

RET is interested in teaching people to live without love and approval if these are not forthcoming. We insist they are not necessary for an adult even though they are highly desirable. And you can be sure when you make that point in a group there is practically always a storm of protest. All the better, because you have got the ball rolling, you have an opportunity to challenge their irrationalities, and that is what the process is all about.

AFTER GROUP SESSIONS

When your group session concludes, it is usually quite beneficial to remove yourself from the room and let the members continue on their own for a half hour or an hour. Do not schedule other groups that follow them, to force this group to end prematurely.

In these leaderless moments the individuals have an opportunity to talk more freely, to compare notes, to help each other out, and to form a cohesiveness and a sense of camaraderie which might bring them together more easily. Many individuals are quite sensitive about coming to counseling in the first place, but if they develop friendships, that makes coming to a group all the easier. If they can remove some of their fears of rejection, their self-consciousness over revealing their problems because they have developed warm contacts among group members, this is all to the good.

A number of groups will continue even after you have disbanded them. They form social ties on their own and will meet at various times. This is really an indication of a successful group because they feel they have gone through some trauma together, have proceeded in their own growth, and identify with one another in a meaningful way. I am always pleased to see this happen and never hesitate to encourage the development of such camaraderie.

A REPEATED ISSUE—ACCEPTING REALITY

One issue that I must deal with repeatedly in group therapy is getting clients to accept reality graciously. It appears that this is indeed one of the assignments which they balk at the most. So self-righteous are they, and so indignant over the many injustices occurring in their lives that they believe a recitation of all the dirty deeds that have been perpetrated upon them is good therapy. They will take endless time to ventilate the unfair situations they have been placed in by an unfeeling society. Many therapists allow the clients to ventilate to their heart's content in the honest belief that when this poison is drained from the group members' system inner peace will be restored.

The worst part of it is that a complaining client usually has a great deal of support from other members of the group who feel that the role of the group is to show understanding for the travails of the other members. I have practically never encountered a group where someone's endless recitation of injustices and wrongdoings was stopped in midair by one of the other group members who had the intelligence to say, "Knock it off and accept life as a pretty unfair place at times." On the contrary, I find that I must make this point practically every time myself. And when I do I usually have a room full of disbelieving and gasping clients who think I am most unfeeling and insensitive.

They tend to retort that I don't understand what they are going through, that if I were in their shoes I would sing a different tune, and that it is only natural to be upset when bad things happen to people as has happened to them. I agree to this latter point quite readily. But then I present the problem of what would happen to them if we all agreed. For example, I suggest what if I agree that they had to be upset because life was unfair, and I got the whole group to agree, and then we all sat around and cried on one another's shoulders over the bad things that were happening to the members of the group? Where would that leave us and what would that get us? Would that remove these damnable afflictions from their lives? Would they have learned how to live with these frustrations because we all had a good cry over them? Would the rotten supervisor or the insensitive mate at home appreciate their dilemma more because we were such a loving group and we held hands and we commiserated with one another at a deep level?

Obviously none of these things would happen. Instead, I try to show them by not accepting their depressions and their complaints about their sad lives that I am doing them an immense service. I have greater respect for them than they have for themselves. I am saying that if they can change the situations in their lives and remove unwanted frustrations, they had better work on these mighty hard. But if these efforts do not accomplish their goals, then the only sound thing they can do is to resign themselves to unfairness, injustice, and to the rotten ups and downs to which all of us are subject. At least by doing that some peace of mind is gained.

When I put the issue in these terms I often find they simply cannot argue against my points and reluctantly, perhaps, begin to realize life is tough and they had better learn to bend with it or else they will crack.

RET theory is applicable not only to individual therapy but to group therapy as well. The comments which I have made in regard to group therapy in no way exclude other things which also apply to the group process. I urge all counselors, who have the opportunity, to practice both types of counseling, both for their own health and for that of their clients.

Chapter 7

Child
Counseling

RET methods applied to children are significantly different from other child therapies just as RET methods for adults differ from other adult therapies. But how so? Simply in that children are regarded as eager learners who already have grasped the beginnings of irrational philosophy by the time they enter counseling. The counselor can teach children as young as five to question these ideas until they experience relief. One instantly notes the similarity between this process and the typical procedure with older subjects.

At this point, however, the similarity ends. Because RET relies on cognitive restructuring, children below the age of five have not matured to the degree that they can understand what is necessary for this kind of counseling. Parents, therefore, almost always join in the therapeutic process to assist in altering or removing frustrations under the recommendations and guidance of the counselor.

This approach to child counseling is quite the opposite from a prevailing assumption that holds: Counseling the child is more important than counseling the parents. According to this view a disturbed child should, in practically all instances, be referred for counseling, since it is the child who has the problem.

This reasoning is fairly sound but it overlooks the important distinction between classical neurotic behavior and misbehavior. Neurotic behavior is characterized primarily by self-pain, i.e., depression or fear. No intention is present to manipulate or to punish others when a behavior is only neurotic. Misbehavior, on the other hand, has as its main purpose the manipulation of others to further one's own interests. Dreikurs has described four goals of misbehavior: attention, power, revenge, and disability (to avoid growth and responsibility) (Dreikurs and Stoltz, 1964).

Both forms of behavior can profit from counseling. Neurotic behavior, to be corrected, certainly requires direct work with the child. But misbehavior can be corrected with or even without the child's being involved in counseling. For the latter, it is perhaps more important how the parents are advised than what the child is told.

Children behave as they do largely because parents and teachers have somehow permitted them to behave objectionably. In the past the emphasis in counseling children was on getting them to understand their behavior and to correct it with the help of the counselor. Although parents were frequently brought into the counseling process, the bulk of the responsibility for the change was placed upon the child.

It is my strong conviction that things go much more swiftly if the opposite approach is taken. I am much more interested in counseling the parents of a difficult child than I am in counseling the child. I do not hesitate to let parents know that I am trying to teach them new methods for dealing with their child because it was their faulty methods in the first place that allowed the child to get out of hand. I then proceed to teach them how not to blame the child but at the same time to be firm. I point out those techniques which reward the child's attention-getting tactics, which make him or her feel infantile, and which scare him or her from growing up. I often spend a lot of time showing them how they are in a power struggle with their children and what they can do about that. In all these attempts I am simply trying to get them to be more educated so that they do not continue with their faulty methods of child-rearing. I find that nothing of much consequence happens in the family until the parents learn new methods.

Of course I see the child as well. Ten to twenty minutes of every half-hour session is spent with the child. I want the child to understand as much as possible about the behavior problem, how it came to be, and what can be done about it. I am, however, aware that my counsel with the child often does no good at all until the teachers and the parents change their behavior. I can talk to the child for a month of Sundays and no change in behavior will occur until those who have authority in the child's life change their tactics. If I can get the parents and the teachers to stop tolerating manipulative actions, then it is much easier for me to explain to the child what is going on, what we can expect to happen if disruptive behavior continues, and what alternatives there are.

In a few rare instances I can counsel a child without reaching the parents at all and get the youngster to see the problem more rationally. Sometimes from these sessions alone the need to change is so clear that no outside pressure is necessary. But this is not the usual course of counseling. The best results invariably come when the authority figures in the child's life have learned more about the dynamic interplay between them and the children and make the necessary alterations in *their* behavior.

RET sees nothing wrong with the counselor's judging as to when to counsel the child alone, with a parent, or together with his or her family. When a case is first brought to my attention I prefer to see the parent briefly, perhaps for about ten minutes of a thirty-minute session.

During this period I try to grasp what the major complaint is. It is a highly structured interview allowing little rambling. Time is short and must be used with the greatest economy.

When I feel content that I know why the parents are seeing me, what their concerns are, and what they are expecting from counseling, I ask to see the child alone.

The boy or girl is then interviewed for the next ten or fifteen minutes. He or she is questioned as to why the interview is taking place. Does the child agree with the parents? If not, what is the child's version? As this probing goes on, I am actively formulating my understanding of the case. It is vital to be sympathetic toward the child at this point. This is no time to come down on the youngster with the heavy hand of rational persuasion. Wait until the soil has been prepared before you expect to reap a rich harvest.

In the remaining minutes the parents are asked to come in again after the youngster is asked to wait in the outer office. I give them my impressions of the general psychological health of the child. They naturally want to know how serious the problem is. If you have bad news to give them, it had better be given by underplaying the problem than by being completely candid. Parents will overplay your interpretation in most cases anyway. It does no harm, therefore, to be conservative.

The windup of this first session should lead to action, to a plan. If psychological testing is sought, now is the time to present that request. The nature, frequency, and length of therapy sessions can now be clarified. I usually ask one parent or both parents to bring the child for the next appointment; I will see the adult or adults briefly again before I see the child. And in the second and all following sessions I will not routinely see the adults again after seeing the child. With those issues agreed upon, the initial interview is over.

Counseling a child with RET challenges another widely held assumption: the counseling method of choice for young children is play therapy. It provides symbolic expression of unconscious problems, ventilation, and high interest for the young participant. For these reasons play therapy has been regarded as a natural and well-suited mode of working with children.

But is it always called for, or even in the majority of instances? Work with RET (Ellis, 1969; Hauck, 1967) has cast grave doubt on this belief. Children as young as five years of age can be reasoned with in precisely the same manner an adult can. You, the counselor, can place a child in a chair opposite you, and fruitful discourse can follow if you will only lower the complexity of your language to suit the needs of the child. With this one exception a child can be taught, debated with, and shown irrationalities of behavior in the same straightforward manner the RET therapists have used with adults.

There is the advantage of its being more to the point, wasting less time, and utilizing teaching, which give verbal therapy a real edge over play therapy. And why can the didactic method not be regarded as a favored technique for counseling children when we realize that it is the most widely used instrument in educating them? The reason it has not been used more widely is simply that our past emphasis in counseling has been experiential rather than cognitive. When the former is appropriate, play therapy is an appropriate method. However, when the resistances have been removed, the present-day therapist considers the job still incomplete. Though the child may feel better, behavior still based on irrational grounds will not change. A cognitive approach attacks these erroneous philosophies head on and will make a lasting modification in behavior if the client chooses to apply this newly learned knowledge.

Play therapy can reveal the fact that a seven-year-old feels guilty when not behaving perfectly. But cognitive therapy shows why it is wrong to feel guilty over that shortcoming, and then goes on to show why it is wrong to blame oneself at *any* time. It is this final step which is so frequently ignored by those therapists who single out play therapy as the obvious method of correction.

OVERCOMING RESISTANCE

The last thing in the world most children want to admit is that they have problems which a therapist has a right to talk about with them. It's not uncommon, therefore, to discover that children will not want to talk about their behaviors at the opening of each session. Worse yet, they often don't know, or forget, or pretend they don't remember what those problems are for which the sessions are being held.

To get around this obstacle I quickly get to the heart of the matter and ask, for example, "Johnny, why are you here?" If the answer is, "I don't know," I do some reminding.

"You're here because you have three habits that are getting you into trouble. Do you remember what they are?"

If again he does not know, or pretends to have forgotten, I supply the answer.

"You lie, you steal, and you goof off. Now, which of these do you want to work on first?"

The question is not made in a derogatory manner since such behavior is not uncommon in children. It is, however, made in a straightforward and matter-of-fact manner.

If Johnny still does not cooperate, I review some of the behaviors his parents are concerned about, and give him an understanding of why such behavior occurs. This usually gets discussion started at which point I can show him how he is irrationally pursuing self-defeating patterns.

For instance, Johnny's lying might be prompted by a bid for additional attention. He knows he'll get caught at it sooner or later and he's unknowingly hoping his parents will make a huge fuss over his untruthfulness. I would then help him see that being noticed by others is not all as important as he makes it (Irrational Idea No. 4).

Of if his lying is prompted by motives of revenge, I try to show him that he is wrong to blame anyone for anything and that anger and hatred are neurotic emotions (Irrational Idea No. 3).

If he lies because he can get away from responsibility momentarily, I focus immediately on his poor self-discipline and how much better off he would be not to lie but to face his difficulties (Irrational Idea No. 7).

You, the counselor, can focus quickly and easily on any of these dynamics if you know them thoroughly and if you can practice what you preach. The latter condition is not absolutely necessary since you can talk a good line and not follow it yourself just as the alcoholic father can validly tell his son not to drink even as he gulps down a beer.

A professional is not in such a forgivable position. Rightly or wrongly people expect their teachers to do what they're teaching. A counselor who is teaching weight control who has a weight problem may be as correct in his counseling as another counselor who does not have. The latter, however, is far more likely to have a favorable impact on his students.

Because I control my weight, run regularly, and continue to turn out about a book a year, people are inclined to listen to me when I speak about self-discipline.

Therefore, to become a good counselor for children *(a)* learn the psychology of rational living and *(b)* set a good model. These two points are good advice in all counseling, not just with children. Generally you do not speak from conviction if you have not mastered RET principles. Even adults will respect your counseling more when they can plainly see how much you have benefited from your own teachings.

DISCIPLINING WITH LOGICAL CONSEQUENCES

Parents will bring problems of disobedience to you more often than all other problems combined. It is imperative that you feel comfortable counseling on this subject or you will seldom be brief or comfortable at your work.

When you are told by parents that a child is not obeying, try to determine *(a)* how severe the problem is, and *(b)* what they have thus far done about it.

If the boy is sixteen years old and is now cursing his mother, walking in and out of the house any time he likes, skipping school, and shoplifting, you know immediately that she has lost considerable control of him and is not likely to regain it without significant help. You may want to counsel her to warn him one more time that another act of disobedience means she'll turn him over to the courts, or place him in foster care, or place him in a reform institution. And then do it!

If the boy won't pick up his room or stop fighting with his sister, or do his homework, it can be assumed milder forms of correction could work.

Parents have three time-honored methods by which to deal with difficult children. When they won't work it is time to use the fourth: logical consequences.

First, let's look at the usual three.

1. *Reasoning, preaching, nagging, and warning.* These are verbal appeals to the child. Parents try to get the child to understand why it is important to be respectful, to pick up one's clothes, to attend classes, and not to shoplift. They try to persuade through logical arguments, ethical principles, religious teachings, or through an appeal to common sense to follow rules.

This is a sound method and is largely responsible for the way values of one generation are passed to the next. Its rightful place in the order of methods to be employed is first. If an appeal to the child's logic does not work, parents must not hesitate to proceed to the next.

2. *Moderate physical control.* Like it or not, many of us are law-abiding because we are afraid to be otherwise. The little fellow keeps his wisecracks to himself when addressing a bully because he wisely fears having his nose rearranged. As long as children have a fear of rejection or physical reprisal from a stronger mother or father they are likely to obey and keep their grumblings to themselves.

Spankings have a valid place in the raising of children, I believe. Physical pain is still one of those very aversive stimuli for which most people have great respect. I see no reason to dismiss it entirely as a means of controlling disobedience.

The problem, however, is that it can get out of hand and it sometimes breeds a backlash. Severe and frequent physical punishment tells us that the program is not working and had better be abandoned because powerful feelings of resentment can be built up. When it does work, it works too well. Children are either cowed so completely into submission that they become afraid of their own shadow and hate themselves, or they adopt the blame philosophy of their tormentor and become hostile persons.

Moderate physical punishment, however, is another matter. Pulling a boy's pants down and spanking him hard enough to make it sting and doing this *several times in his life* may be all that is ever needed to remind him to respect his parents. If he fears his parents (along with loving them), so much the better. I doubt that parents can love an authority that they don't respect. And a large percentage of respect is ultimately respect for power and the way the parents can translate that into good or bad for the child. A youngster who does not fear, in the slightest, the power parents can use against him lives in a state of anarchy.

Therefore, when you counsel parents who ask if it is permissible to swat the child who seriously steps out of line, the answer is in the affirmative. A woman once told me her daughter didn't like an order she was given and called my client a bad name.

"What should I have done? I was so completely shocked and stunned," she said.

"You could have smacked her across the mouth quickly and hard," I advised.

And I meant it. If parents don't act decisively at such moments, they set a precedent they'll soon regret.

WARNING: I never advocate severe physical beatings unless the parent is literally doing so in self-defense. Otherwise we create a generation of masochists or sadists.

But *infrequent, moderate,* and appropriately timed physical punishment, that's something different.

3. *Penalties.* These sometimes work wonderfully. Too often, however, they bomb out and the parents are left puzzled, wondering what happened.

The problem with most penalties is that they are irrelevant. The child fails to see the connection between his misdeed and the penalty. The teenage boy can't have the car because he didn't clean his room. What does one have to do with the other? he asks. The conclusion he arrives at is that his parents aren't really *trying to teach him a thing,* only *punish* him. He may react to the punishment with additional defiance but might have accepted it if he thought he was genuinely being taught something for his own good.

4. *Logical consequences.* Rudolf Dreikurs offered us the concept of logical consequences (Dreikurs and Stoltz, 1964). This principle states that a penalty should teach a child something about the offense so the child will learn how injurious

the behavior is to others and to oneself. The penalty is much better if it *makes sense* and is *not done out of spite.* Children can easily see the difference between a penalty that is meant to get revenge and one that is meant to make a point.

For instance, if a son fails repeatedly to buckle up his seat belt, the father might first advise him as to why that's a sound procedure. If that doesn't work after a few such episodes, Dad discontinues the sermonizing and resorts the very next time to a logical consequence: he doesn't start the car. If the son wants to know why they're not moving, Dad can tell him they will as soon as he's safely strapped in. When he's buckled up, Dad starts the car *without another word.*

Be sure the parents see why this is called a *logical consequence.* The son easily sees why he is sitting in the driveway: *he* is not being careful, and he is indirectly keeping the car from moving. The choice was his. If he doesn't like being late, he can change the situation easily enough any moment he chooses. He can buckle up. *But he doesn't have to.* And therein lies the beauty of this method.

He is told he does not *have* to clean up his room. However, the consequence is that he won't be allowed to have his boy friend join him there.

He is told he had better eat his breakfast or he will not get a ride to school. His body requires fuel to start off a hard day of learning. Mother wouldn't send him across town in a car with only a gallon of gas, would she? So, if he wants to go to school that day and be on time, he had better eat a nourishing and leisurely breakfast. Otherwise he will stay home. And that's okay too. Mother will accept it either way, since she knows he likes school and would be bored at home. What if the child wants to stay home? Use another consequence.

THE POWER STRUGGLE

This occurs from ages one or two all the way up to adulthood. In such a struggle the child is trying to prove that he or she is more powerful than the adult. At the same time the adult is trying to prove the opposite. However, when you ask the parents, "Who do you think is the more powerful?" they almost always say, "Why, we are of course."

This is the time at which you point out that the child is the more powerful. The child can be so intent on winning the power struggle that he doesn't care what price he must pay to prove he is more powerful. He does this at great cost to his present and future happiness. Regardless, he is so determined on being victorious over his parents that no price is too great to pay for their defeat.

How, for example, can a parent make a child study? He can be sent to his room, surely. But will he study? Can't he daydream the whole while and lie about having read his assignment? How ultimately powerless parents are!

Parents can make their daughter go to school, but they can't make her stay. The moment Mother drives away she can leave the school grounds too. And any time she decides she doesn't want to graduate she can get into a series of difficulties that force the school authorities to expel her. And if they won't, she can always get pregnant.

Wise? Of course not. But it proves her point. She *is* more powerful. Then how are parents to control and guide their children? Are they totally powerless?

Certainly not. And this is material you, the counselor, will want to memorize and digest. Advise your bewildered mothers and fathers to *extricate* themselves from the power struggle. Advise the following: "Do not match your authority against your children's stubbornness because they can drive you up the wall with their spiteful and self-defeating behavior. Instead, *give them a choice*. And tell them what you think the consequences will be for each. Recommend, don't order them to study, get in early, brush their teeth, etc. Then let them choose and either reap the rewards for a sound choice or suffer the consequences for a foolish choice. The experience, because *they were in control,* will have a strong impact and it is hoped will induce a wiser behavior *next time.*"

The beauty of this program is that the parent doesn't wind up being the heavy. The parent did not make the boy come late to the game. The boy did. It was *his* choice not to buckle his seat belt and thus delay the trip. The parent was not directly involved. The parent was content to let him bring about either result he desired. It was his choice and now *the problem is his too.*

When you explain this technique to parents it will dawn on them that you are advising them to let their children make some rather serious mistakes in the hope that the children will learn from those errors. They will insist that they are counseling with you to prevent those mistakes being made in the first place.

They want you to *prevent* the boy from dropping out of school, buying drugs, coming in after ten P.M., or avoiding his chores. And here you are telling them to let these things happen. Why should they spend money for that sort of advice? they'll ask you. Do you have a good answer?

I suggest you point out that the child refuses to be reasonable, saying: "There is a power struggle going on, and your child is making you look foolish. So, throw up your hands and accept it *since you can't prevent it anyway.* Instead, explain: *(a)* what choices there are, *(b)* what the consequences will be for each choice, and *(c) let your child suffer with the results.*"

Harsh reality will soon enough reinforce what you were trying to teach. The more it stings the more quickly the lesson may be learned. Granted that's a painful way to learn, but for some it's the only way.

This method will not necessarily prevent a sixteen-year-old from quitting school or eloping. And the fact that it may take four years to regret an earlier indiscretion does not mean you have failed to teach a good lesson. At twenty one is still young and has ample opportunity to make the most of past mistakes.

The child corrected with logical consequences early in life will usually benefit in two ways:

1. By getting hurt so often through ignoring parental advice, the child will learn to have enormous respect for parental counsel.

2. By making many errors one is exposed to the decision-

making process. In time, because of the feedback that experience provides, one tends to become a skilled decision maker.

THE ATTENTION GETTER

The Adlerians have properly focused on attention-getting as one of the most frequent problems children give adults. Their test for the presence of attention vs. a power struggle is classic. For example, if the teacher tells Bobby to stop drumming his fingers in class, and he stops, only to resume shortly thereafter, you can count on Bobby's having a problem with wanting too much attention. However, if the teacher tells Bobby to stop drumming his fingers and he then does so with both hands, that's a power struggle.

Attention-getting is best handled if it is ignored. Counsel the parents: "Step over your daughter rolling on the floor in a temper tantrum. If that is impractical, put her in a room until she quiets down. If she yells while in the room, do not tell her to be quiet. That is not ignoring her, and she will take courage from your yelling because she's getting attention after all."

Advise the parents: "Don't spank an attention getter. Don't sit down for a two-hour heart-to-heart talk with an attention getter. Don't yell at the child. These are all ways of giving her the attention she thinks she'll die if she does not get." You may wonder why any intelligent child would want such painful attention. The parents will even ask you about it. They have a tendency to feel guilty over possibly having neglected the child.

I usually point out that neglect is not the motive behind attention-getting; it is expectation based on past performance. Attention getters have often had excessive attention and have learned to love it. That's why they don't want to share it and that's why they aren't fussy about the condition of the attention.

Sometimes I elaborate the point in this way: adults always want more money even if they have plenty. I ask the parents if they would accept a gift of a million dollars if I convinced them I could afford it. They agree they'd accept it. I then ask if they would accept another million even though they now have plenty of money. Practically all of them would accept. I then ask if they would accept these funds if the bills were dirty, torn, or wet. And again they are delighted to have the money.

In this way I hope to make the point that attention getters are not usually starved for attention. The parents have not been negligent. Rather, the time has come to ignore the attention getter and train the child to get along on less.

DISABILITY

The child who is afraid to grow up will indicate this by regressing, by using illness, and by denying strengths as further proof of his or her right to be pampered and not pushed into growth. Watch for the child who baby-talks after the birth of a sibling. Watch for the youngster who gets stomachaches before leaving for school. Watch for the child who frequently says, "I can't." That boy wants to be bathed, to have his shoes tied, his meat cut, and his hair brushed. When you see these symptoms you are dealing with a child who is trying to convince his parents he is weak and disabled and does not want to do grown-up things.

One of the better ways of curing this condition is simply not to help the child too much. Advise the parents: "If he won't cut his meat (and you believe he is perfectly capable of doing so), let him pick it up with his hands. He'll get so frustrated and messy in time that he'll attempt the task." The moaning and groaning that goes along with this learning is for the parents' benefit and can safely be ignored.

Counsel the parents: "If he wants to stay home because he's ill, accept his diagnosis and then put him to bed all day without benefit of books, radio, or television. If he gets no secondary gains for his illness, he may prefer to accept responsibility instead." Pitying the child is the great danger to which the parents had better be alert. To be too kind to a frightened child does him no service. Pity is immediately detected by the youngster and is used to his full advantage. Eventually this is unsatisfactory to both the child and the parents.

A TYPICAL BRIEF COUNSELING SESSION WITH PARENTS AND CHILD

THERAPIST: What seems to be the problem with nine-year-old Roger?

He: His sharp tongue and dirty looks. He is basically immature but he is very verbal. He could talk you out of your shirt.

T: What happens when you tell him to do something?

He: A big sigh or a huff.

She: He will turn around and give you a smart answer. He stomps. All the way up stairs you can hear him. He'll get in his closet and he'll throw things. We can't send him to his room for punishment. We've got a small house. He wants to go to that room, like on a Saturday. I don't really know he is there. He likes to watch cartoons and be by himself. You don't have any trouble as long as you don't ask him to do anything. If we go in the car, he is down and I say, "What's the matter with you?" He says, "I get carsick every time I go in the car." Well, not if it is going somewhere he wants to go. He is not in the least sick.

T: That's his way of showing a protest, is it?

She: Yes. And at suppertime, I have seen times it would be an hour and a half and he is still sitting there with the same meat and vegetables. He'll take maybe a small piece of meat.

T: About as big as a quarter?

She: Yes. He has four little blobs there on his plate and he will sit there. He is smart enough to know it just ruins the whole supper. I am sure that is why he is doing it. We know he has manipulated us, but we don't know what to do about it.

T: You say you have a small house. How small?

He: It's a split-level.

T: Do you have an empty room in the house where you could put him if you needed to?

He: The bathroom would be about the only place. We have used the bathroom as a time-out room. We'll have him go in there and sit and not play in the water.

She: He'll kick, he'll bang. He wants you to know where he is. He can keep your attention. He can keep you going.

T: You have something there you want me to look at? I see, a study done on the boy in August?

She: He was originally sent to Big City. He was tested for preschool when he was three and Dr. D. sent him to Big City when he was three and a half.

T: For hyperactivity? And was he put on medication?

He: We tried several things. Ritalin was one. We discovered coffee as a more or less depressant to quiet him down in the car when we went on vacation. He is verbal. He will just drive you nuts.

T: I notice that he has a full-scale I.Q. of 123. That's not bad.

She: He had been put in a gifted program as far as language and math are concerned.

T: Is he still on medication now?

She: No.

T: When was he taken off?

She: Probably in 1975 was the last time. Personally I don't like the medication. There wasn't that much difference with him on it.

He: I would rather have him worked up a little bit than be on a drug. It slowed him down.

T: Okay. We have been talking about ten minutes and I want to see the boy a little while and I'll call you back in and give you my impressions and we'll see where we go from there. Okay?

(The parents leave and Roger is asked to come in.)

T: Have a seat, would you, please? Tell me, Roger, what seems to be the problem?

C: With what?

T: Well, with things at home? Why did your parents bring

you to me? Why are you here to see me? (He shrugs his
shoulders.) You don't know?

C: I don't know. They didn't tell me.

T: What do you think the reason is?

C: I don't know that either.

T: What grade are you in?

C: Third.

T: What kind of grades do you make?

C: A's and B's most of the time.

T: How do you get along at home?

C: Pretty good.

T: Any kind of difficulty?

C: Not many.

T: What are some of the difficulties? You are here because
your folks are having some trouble with you. Did you
know that?

C: No.

T: Yes. They want to know what we can do about it. So I
thought: "Well, let me talk to the young man and see what
the problem is. Let me see what we can do about some of
these problems." You know what they are saying?

C: No, I don't know.

T: Well, they are saying such things as you have to have the
last word in everything. They put you in a room and you
kick and you fuss. Whatever they tell you to do you do the
opposite. Are you aware of that?

C: Yes.

T: Tell me about that.

C: I don't always get in trouble.

T: Tell me about some of those times when you and the
family have a fight or when there is a lot of yelling about
something. Tell me about some of the bad times.

C: Well, I'm supposed to have a bath every other night and
sometimes I don't have one every other night. My mother
gets mad at me. And sometimes when I don't set the table
and when I don't empty the wastebaskets . . .

T: What does she do?

C: She gets mad at me.

T: What do you do?

C: Well . . .

T: Talk back?

C: Sometimes.

T: What do you say?

C: I just talk back.

T: They seem to think that you have a smart mouth. That means you are sort of fresh.

C: What does fresh mean?

T: Rude. You are not respectful to your elders.

C: Sometimes.

T: Is it hard for you to be respectful to your elders?

C: No.

T: Then why don't you do it?

C: I don't know that I am being rude.

T: Oh, I see. Well, do you answer in a very loud way, a smart-aleck way?

C: Sometimes.

T: Why?

C: That's just the way I talk.

T: I see. Do you feel that they hem you in too much? They don't give you enough freedom? Dictate to you too much?

C: I don't think that they do that all the time.

T: Well, a lot of times children will do the sort of things you are doing for one of four reasons. One of the reasons is that they want a lot of attention. Maybe you are sassing back, acting up, yelling, and all that kind of stuff so you will get more attention from your mother and father.

   Another reason is that you want to show them that you are more powerful than they are. So when they tell you to turn right you turn left and say to yourself, "You just try to make me turn right." Or they say, "I want you to eat," then you don't eat. They can't make you eat. Or, "I want you to go to bed and go to sleep," and they can't make you go to sleep so you are going to deliberately stay awake.

C: I don't always deliberately stay awake. It just takes me a long time to get to sleep.

T: Well, I just used that as an example. See, if you are trying to show them that you are more powerful than they are, then you are in a power struggle. Maybe that's the other reason why you might be having trouble with them. You are trying to prove to them that they are not strong enough to make you do one thing or the other.

And the third reason is that you want to get even with them. Revenge. You don't like what they have done to you, so you say: "Hey, I'm going to get back at you. You tell me to do something and I'm going to do the opposite. I'm going to try to hurt you." That's revenge.

The fourth one is called weakness, or sickness, or disability. That's where you are trying to show them: "Hey, listen. Leave me alone. Don't make me do adult things, grown-up things. I want to remain childish. I want to remain a baby. And if you expect too much from me, why then I will have to do more and more things. And I don't want to do that. I want to remain a child. I can't do all these things you are asking me to do. So leave me alone. Let me remain a child. I don't want to grow up. I feel disabled. I feel sick. I feel weak. I can't cut my meat. I can't tie my shoes. I can't go to school today. I'm sick." You see the weakness? That's another reason. It's called disability. Now, there they are—the four reasons: (1) you want attention, (2) you want power, (3) you want revenge, (4) you want to remain a child. Which of those four might fit what you are doing?

C: Part of three of them.

T: Which ones?

C: The first three.

T: Okay. That's a good thought. In other words, sometimes you are doing it for attention and power and revenge.

C: Yes.

T: Do you mind if we talk some more sometime about why you are doing these things? Maybe we can help you not use these methods to get attention. Maybe I can show you why you don't have to go into a power struggle with your folks. Or how you might get over your anger and revenge.

Would you care if we talked again so I can show you how to handle these problems a little differently?

C: I don't care.

T: Do you think you have a problem? Or do you think your folks have a problem?

C: I don't think either of us have a problem.

T: You think you don't have a problem and they don't have a problem?

C: Yes.

T: Okay. Are you eating okay? Sleeping okay?

C: Yes.

T: Do you have friends?

C: Yes.

T: How many friends do you have?

C: Quite a few.

T: How many?

C: Well, the whole class full.

T: But are they all personal friends?

C: What do you mean by personal?

T: Well, not everybody that you know is your friend. Those are acquaintances. Real close acquaintances are called friends.

C: Yes, some in my class aren't exactly friends.

T: Yes, but you have, say, three, four, five friends?

C: I'd say maybe six.

T: Okay. What is the biggest thing that irritates you about your mother and your father?

C: That they yell at me.

T: Why do they yell at you?

C: They tell me that they yell at me because they want me to be good.

T: Then what do you do when they yell at you?

C: Sort of get mad.

T: How do you show that? Do you kick and scream? Or do you say nasty things to them? How do you show it?

C: Sometimes I make faces and sometimes I walk off.

T: And that's where you get the last word. Right?

C: Sometimes. Sometimes I just walk off and go into my room and shut the door.

T: You like your room?

C: I like my room.

T: You have all your toys there?

C: Yes.

T: Okay. Now let me talk to your folks. Okay?

C: Okay.

(Roger leaves and I ask his folks in.)

He: Did you learn anything?

T: Did I learn anything? I think the impression I had before I saw him is largely substantiated. He's a cute little fellow. He's bright. He's somewhat on his guard.

He: I don't know about anybody else, but he can read us like a book. He is very observant.

T: Okay. Here's what I did. I said: "Look, the kind of behavior that you are showing at home is usually prompted by four goals. Children do this sort of thing for four reasons. One is that they want a lot of attention, secondly they want to prove that they are more powerful than their parents, thirdly they want revenge because they are mad at their parents for some reason, or they want to convince the parents that they are helpless little kids and therefore too much cannot be expected from them because they don't want to grow up." I said, "Which of these applies to you?" And he said, "The first three." In other words, he is saying, "Sometimes I misbehave for attention, for power, and for revenge." So then I have to counsel you and him in terms of teaching him how to change and teaching you how to deal with him when he comes along with some attention-getting behavior or because he wants to show you that you are not powerful enough to make him do whatever you want or because he wants to get even with you because he is mad at you.

He: Someone suggested we ignore him.

She: The teacher can't ignore it at school. He makes a shambles out of the whole classroom. She can't ignore it.

T: That's right.

She: He says to me, "You scream at me all the time." I said, "Roger, I can ask you to do something three times," and he does not hear at all. The only time he does anything is when I yell.

T: I think you had better learn how to handle him without screaming and yet be firm at the same time. By letting him suffer certain consequences when he behaves badly or by putting him into a time-out situation where he gets no satisfaction or pleasure might have an eventual effect on him. You are saying that the only room in your house is the bathroom. All right, then keep him in the bathroom, and if he kicks and fusses or yells, tell him that he is going to stay in five minutes more. If he yells louder, then add another five minutes. He'll learn there is nothing to be gained by yelling. And don't yell through the door, "Now I told you what was going to happen and I told you you shouldn't do this." Don't carry on a conversation with him. That would be self-defeating, too, because that's attention.

She: Any kind, bad or good, either one.

T: He'll take any kind. He is so hungry for it. He thinks he has to have it, which he doesn't at all.

She: Well, you know he gets so much. We are drained.

T: He wants attention not because he is not getting enough but just because he likes it. He's not a deprived little youngster. He's got good, loving parents and that's fine. But he simply wants more attention. He is an only child. He doesn't really know how to share. So he is going to do whatever he can to get your attention and to bug you, and so on.

She: He doesn't play with the other kids, you know. He says it's their fault. He'll come home crying and I say: "You can't cry. You're nine." If they see him cry, they will know Roger is a soft touch.

He: He's emotional.

T: Okay, I don't think this should take a long time. We can work together every two or three weeks. Let me instruct you on some of the finer points of how to handle his problem and how not to fall into the traps he sets for you. He sort of baits you.

He: Yes, he has.

T: Sure he has. He's done that a lot of times. I want you to ignore it as much as possible. Put him in the bathroom.

She: But his smart mouth is the worst thing.

T: The smart-mouthing is for your benefit. He thinks, "If I smart-mouth, you're going to react and I'm going to demonstrate my control over you and I'll get a lot of attention." When he smart-mouths just put your spoon down if you're mixing up a bowl of something, take him by the arm, don't say a thing, put him in the bathroom and if he comes out, get a lock on the outside and lock it, if he won't stay in by just telling him. Don't keep telling him why he is going into time out. When he smart-mouths—in he goes!

She: What if we are away? Like at my folks he'll just make a shambles.

T: Send him outside, or put him in the bathroom there, or put him in the car if it is good weather, or something like that. In other words you want to show him you are not going to fall for this anymore and he is not going to continue to manipulate you. I want this stopped.

She: It has to be because he is going to be getting big and we won't be able to do a thing with him.

T: Exactly. Well, now, I've seen a lot of cases like this and I see no reason why we can't alter this if you follow my thinking and if you are patient and consistent. Both of you have to do the same thing. If you can do that, I don't see why this problem should last very long. You'll see some changes within a matter of months if you start applying yourself and letting him see that when he steps out of line he is going to be one mighty lonely kid and all the yelling and screaming in the world isn't going to change a thing until he shapes up. That's the stage we want to get to. All your lovely sermons are for nothing because that's what he wants. He wants another lecture from you, so don't give him the lecture. Give him the isolation. Then let's see what happens. I want to have another appointment with all three of you or with one of you and the boy.

He: Great.

Chapter 8

Hard-Learned Lessons

In this chapter I want to share a number of random ideas that have occurred to me about effective counseling. These insights arise out of my personal experiences and represent techniques I have found helpful. Study them carefully and apply them judiciously. I believe they will prove worthy of the effort.

EXPECT TO BE MISQUOTED

People hear what they want to hear and forget what they disagree with. This is never truer than within the counseling relationship. Therefore, expect people to return to their homes and say that their counselor said that mother was all wrong, husband was an alcoholic, the client ought to give them all an ultimatum, or that father had a perfect right to smack the family around in order to get them into shape.

The worst part of it is that frequently the other people hearing these supposed quotes will believe that you did in fact make those statements. Let your clients know that they may in fact do that and ask them not to. Suggest to the client: "Look, when you get home don't tell your family that I said your wife ought to be locked up. Tell them that, based on what you told me, she appears to be a troubled person and perhaps needs to be hospitalized. Try not to misquote me, please, by telling your wife I think she is out of her mind. Okay?"

The technique of alerting the client to the fact that *he or she is responsible for the opinion that you have of the people he or she talks about* is extremely important. It is always wise for you to say that, in view of the information your client is giving you, you have the right to make certain conclusions. You yourself, however, do not know that these conclusions are correct. You are only basing these conclusions on the assumption that your client is reporting the facts to you correctly. And if they are correct, then these are some of the statements you can make. Therefore, caution the client not to go home and quote you directly but to quote you only in the context that you, the counselor, made statements based on the information that was given to you by the client. And then you can even add the caution at the end, "And if you do quote me out of context, I'll deny it."

This is no academic point by any means. It is a very important one because it frequently happens that when you have heard a member of the family being run down by your client and you get a mental picture of that person you may be very surprised next week when you are able to talk to that person. You may be looking at a perfectly delightful human being. And to have taken your client's side against that person without having had a chance to make your own evaluation is truly unfair. In numerous instances I was relieved by covering my tracks when I cautioned the client with whom I was talking that the statements I made were based solely on his or her interpretation and the information he or she supplied. And wouldn't you know it, when I was able to see that other person, I changed my mind dramatically.

Although you are sworn to confidentiality, your client is not. If you let certain opinions slip through about persons or events, you can bet your bottom dollar that you are going to be quoted by your client to someone in the community. This could lead to embarrassment and even a lawsuit if you are not careful. I very strongly caution you to be distrustful of your clients in this regard even though they may not purposely sabotage your efforts.

DON'T ACCEPT HISTORY AS AN EXCUSE

The client who says, "But my husband drinks because his father beat him," and the client who says, "My child sasses me because he doesn't have a father and I am trying to make up for him," are missing the point. They are seeing you because they are unhappy over some symptomatic behavior on the part of other people. If that's the case, then one of the best ways to bring relief to the situation is to get those other people to change their objectionable behavior. A historical reason for behavior is no ground for letting it continue. My tactic, therefore, is usually to point out to them that I don't want to hear any excuses, that I don't care how unhappy the person was in the past. He is being a pain in the neck now, and if you, the client, want more happiness you'd better do something about the problem. *What we want in dealing with others is change, not an explanation* as to why the problem exists in the first place. Every problem exists for some good reason, but that doesn't mean that we have to tolerate it.

I once had a serious quarrel with a co-worker who interviewed a young man who was sent to jail over the weekend. He shot up the town after he was rejected by his girl friend. The co-worker felt that counseling was necessary for him and that we needn't get tough with him because he now understood why the young man was so upset. Apparently the young man had not had a very loving mother and he was reacting with the same rage against the rejection by his girl friend as he did when he was repeatedly rejected by his mother.

I took a different view of the matter by insisting that the boy's sitting in jail for a couple of weeks would make the point very nicely that I didn't give a hoot what his reasons for shooting up the town were. All I was interested in was seeing that the shooting stopped and I was not going to excuse it on the basis that he was a neglected little boy. That wasn't something I could help nor could he. He was going to have to learn to live with that sad fact of life and to straighten up and fly right regardless.

This is a hard-nosed attitude. I don't apologize for it because I find it produces growth. Those counselors who want to mollycoddle their clients by excusing inconsiderate behavior toward others on the grounds of past frustrations are only asking for more misbehavior. Life is unfair and even though you were treated unkindly at one time, you still have no moral right to take your disturbances out on other people.

BE TRUTHFUL TO YOUR CLIENTS
AND PROTECT CONFIDENTIALITY

In counseling, confidentiality is the best policy unless you have been permitted by your client to release a piece of information. A man who comes in and says that he has had four affairs but doesn't want you to tell his wife is asking for confidentiality. The teenage boy who comes for drug counseling may not mind if you tell his parents that he has been smoking pot but strongly insists that you do not tell his folks about his shooting up heroin.

I remember to hold such confidences by writing them down in my notes in the client's folder and then putting a line through them. In this way I have the information for my own use but won't slip up and read it accidentally to the other party.

I have a high regard for the confidentiality of my clients and can and want to assure them that if they speak to me of private matters, the information will remain between us and no one else. This is not only a practical attitude, it is an ethical one as well. Aside from those two considerations, however, there is always a third: the legal issues of which we had better be cognizant. In our litigious society you have only to look cross-eyed at someone and you may have a lawsuit slapped on you. Silence is the better part of wisdom in a society of hungry lawyers and angry clients.

On many occasions the decision for the counselor is not whether to reveal or not reveal a confidence, but whether to tell the client something that would prove your total honesty but not help the client much in the process. Shall you tell your female client that her husband was fined fifty dollars for drunken driving last night? She is already depressed and heartbroken. Perhaps delaying the news until she is calmer would be the kinder solution.

Or is it helpful to tell Joe's parents that he hates them? They could feel crushed at such total rejection. Would a diplomatic phrasing be better even though it would not convey the boy's truest feelings?

My rule of thumb in such instances is to ask myself whether the clients are capable of tolerating the truth. If I think they are strong enough to do so and will not pass out if they hear something they find distasteful, then I do not hesitate to inform them. If, however, I suspect that they would be shattered by the information, I withhold it until such time that I think they are strong enough to absorb it. Should they ask me about this information before I think they are ready to handle it, I give it in as gentle a way as I possibly can. And if at that point they become distrubed, I regret the fact that I had to do what they asked me to but I do not disturb myself over it since that is their problem, not mine. And after all, that is why they are in counseling: because they have a tendency to disturb themselves.

THAT SPECIAL REMARK

The RET therapist usually throws out a number of ideas in any particular counseling session in the hope that all of them will eventually have some impact on the client. As logical as that may be it turns out often that clients are not moved by every logical argument you give. They are sometimes moved by a single, powerful argument that is terribly relevant to them and that changes their whole approach to their problems. I remember once talking to a woman about her husband's behavior. She was ready to give him up to another woman because of several irritating traits. I pointed out that the other woman would reap the benefits of all the work she had been doing to improve his manners.

Several years later when I talked to her at a social occasion she said: "I'll never forget that remark you made when I was in your office. Remember when you told me that if I gave up on trying to get my husband to change, that another woman would simply benefit from all the work that I had done? Well, that did it. No woman was going to come in and get the benefits of all the work I had put into this marriage. No, sir!"

Do not hesitate to use a shotgun approach rather than a rifle approach. A bullet is one unit and either it hits the mark or it doesn't. Throw out a dozen or more arguments against the client's irrationalities in the hope that perhaps one will hit the target. You will find that often it is the total impact of these arguments that does the job.

GIVE OCCASIONAL EXAMPLES FROM YOUR PRACTICE AND FROM YOUR LIFE

It really helps to let your clients hear how the information you are giving them has worked for you. The assumption is that if it is good enough for you, it might be good enough for them also. I would caution you not to overdo this practice because it can become mighty boring listening to somebody's life history visit after visit. They are not there to hear about your tales, after all, they are there for you to listen to theirs. But, when you can throw in an example from your own experience that makes an important point, I see no reason why you cannot pull from this experience.

Some clients sought me out about discipline in writing books. In each case I went into detail in how I managed to get my books written and encouraged them to follow suit. One person finished a master's thesis, and several social workers got their papers in on time largely because of the inspiration which I believe I supplied.

REVIEWING PROGRESS

One of the first questions to ask on visits subsequent to the initial session is how the client is doing. If the client says that things are better, I usually respond that I am delighted to hear so, but I then ask, "Why?"

This question often surprises my clients because they wonder why they should analyze something that seems to be working so well. Yet I find that such progress is short-lived unless they have a clear understanding of what they have been doing to make matters better. Improvement does not usually come haphazardly. It is often the result of diligent effort and practice. The good feelings that result are a logical payoff from this effort. The clients who do not understand what they have been doing are much more likely to falter and lose ground the next time they are confronted with the same frustrations.

Let me cite excerpts from a letter that was written to me recently. I had met this person at a workshop and as I was passing her she very pleasantly said, "Hello, Paul." I turned and saw a very trim and attractive woman who seemed to know me, but I didn't know her. She smiled as though she recognized my bewilderment and then told me who she was. It turned out that she was an acquaintance of mine whom I had had in therapy a couple of years before and who in fact lived not far from me. But she had lost so much weight that I simply did not recognize her. I asked her how she had possibly lost so much weight and she couldn't answer. I then cautioned her during our conversation that she could give it some thought or she might find herself putting on weight again. Unless she understood how she achieved that control, she might find herself losing it.

Some weeks later she wrote the following letter:

Dear Paul:

Since you were interested in my recent transformation I thought I would write down some comments on why and how it took place and some of the aftereffects. I'm writing them for my own clarification as well as to try to explain them to you.

What motivated me to go from 300 pounds to 155 pounds in the last year:

1. I must have felt unconsciously I was ready to do it since my remarriage in 1978. I have felt happier, more secure, and more confident in general.

2. I think everyone must have a point where something he doesn't like bothers him enough that he must do something about it.

3. I thought I might have to look for another job and would be turned down because of my size. I feel it is necessary for me to work for both psychological and financial reasons.

4. We're moving to the suburbs. I want to be active in gardening and sports and realized I would be physically unable to do this at 300 pounds.

5. My size was becoming a problem as far as finding large enough chairs. Those chairs which were large enough often creaked when I sat down and it was a constant fear I would embarrass myself by actually demolishing a chair.

6. I was constantly tired and sleepy.

7. I was acutely aware that my enormous size was causing many people to openly stare at me, a very uncomfortable feeling.

8. It was becoming increasingly difficult to find clothing to fit me.

In general I was totally dissatisfied with my appearance. I hardly had the energy to do my job, my housework, take part in making love, become involved in recreational activities, etc.

How did I do it? I did it one day at a time (never did it that way before). I counted calories, approximately 700 calories a day. I ate only foods I liked, particularly large quantities of low-calorie foods I enjoyed. After I lost 100 pounds I exercised approximately four to five times a week for an hour. The exercise helped firm me up and gave me added energy—a real feeling of well-being.

Benefits from my weight loss:

1. Self-concept high.

2. Enjoy increased admiration and respect of my husband.

3. Increased energy which led to new interest.

4. Great sex life.

5. Enjoy compliments of friends, co-workers, and children.

6. Have a real feeling of major accomplishment.

7. Enjoying clothes.

The only advice I can give to those who are overweight is: somehow you must know when the time is right for you, find a food plan to suit your individual needs (amounts, types of foods, and frequency and times of eating).

I don't think I could have overcome my problem of overweight

if you hadn't helped me learn to overcome depression. Again thanks
for all you taught me.

From a formerly fat depressive

I don't suppose that all clients you ask to analyze their
improvement will go into this kind of detail. However, in
your following sessions it is important that they show some
insight into why improvement has occurred.

In a similar vein it is also wise to get the clients to recall
the times when they could have acted quite irrationally but
did not. Did they, for example, encounter any frustrations
over which they would have ordinarily gotten angry but this
time controlled themselves? Yes? Then how did they manage
to do so? Did some sad thing happen in their lives for which
they would have ordinarily felt sorry for themselves? If it did,
then how did they manage not to do so?

It is important to go into these situations in some depth
because it lets the clients realize that they had considerable
success. They learn thereby that they encountered a number
of situations which could have caused untold frustration and
provoked disturbances but because of their previous session
were able to avoid them. This lets them know that they *were*
doing their homework and, in fact, under their own power
avoided a number of neurotic reactions.

I sometimes go into three or four of these situations during
a session to let the clients see for themselves how well they
have done. It can surprise and delight them how many situations they avoided which ordinarily would have created serious problems. And lastly, it shows them in no unmistaken
way that they avoided problems because they, and only they,
reacted to their life problems differently. These changes did
not happen by magic or because they took medicine, or because their girl friend or boyfriend went out with them. The
changes happened because they thought about their problem
differently and worked hard at them.

UNCONSCIOUS PROBLEMS AS RED HERRINGS

Every so often when you try to get your client to understand why a member of his or her family is behaving strangely you will find that your interpretations and your best rational efforts are not getting anywhere. What seems to be the problem in such cases? Often your client believes there is an unconscious problem in the person he or she is having trouble with and that unconscious problem has not been discovered. When the therapist uncovers that problem everything will be well. For example, a woman was lonely, felt rejected, had no companionship from her husband, and was giving him a bad time for it. I told him this repeatedly but he kept insisting that the problem was not his, it was his wife's. She had an unconscious problem with being unable to enjoy life, and if that problem were explored farther, I would absolutely see that he was not involved.

Another example is of a man whose wife did not love him. Again I suggested certain obvious changes he could make if he wanted his marriage repaired. He simply did not get the message, would not make a few simple changes, and his wife became increasingly disenchanted with the marriage. It was because he had the feeling that she had some unconscious problem which we had simply not probed and as soon as I would find it everything would fit nicely into place.

These are actually resistances. Both of these gentlemen were fighting against change. They would have loved for there to be a deep unconscious problem because that would have saved them from needing to change. It would permit them to sit back and say: "You change. You have a problem. I am totally innocent of what is happening in the family."

Do not accept this line of reasoning. When you have your dynamic formulation clearly in mind, press for that. Help the client to face the possibility that he may be hoping for an unconscious problem to exist so that it gets him away from the hard work which is called for on his part.

One of the ways to accomplish this is to tell the client that he could give your thinking a reasonable chance to work. If, for example, his wife claims she is lonely, let us see what happens to her emotions when he provides her with a great deal more of his company. If you are correct, your interpretation will hold up and he will have to acknowledge it. If you are incorrect, you can always say he may have been correct and perhaps other avenues could be explored.

I TRIED WHAT YOU SAID, BUT IT DIDN'T WORK

As an RET therapist you frequently give advice and from time to time your client will come back to you and say: "I tried what you said, but it didn't work. Now what?"

If you are not prepared, this kind of attack can set you right back in your chair. The client is putting the total responsibility for his or her changing and emotional life in your hands, and wants you to come up with a magical solution and prove that what you were suggesting was not effective.

Do not get caught in this trap. Instead, immediately ask the client, "Well, why didn't you make my suggestion work?" or "What did you do that prevented my advice from working?" In other words, make *the client* responsible for not showing any movement since the last session. Don't automatically assume the responsibility. Chances are you are right and the client is wrong. Therefore, ask the client to tell you in some detail what happened and listen for the obvious flaws in the client's handling of the problem at the home front. Then advise the client to go back and try again and to *make* your advice work.

The usual reasons for clients' lack of progress stem from their poor self-discipline in questioning the soundness of their irrational beliefs. Chances are they have not spent five consecutive minutes disputing with themselves. And they wonder why your instruction hasn't changed them into a corporate president.

Or clients will admit that you make sense. "But it's *so hard* to put your instruction into practice." This provides a convenient rationalization for not progressing.

In some cases, especially among the self-pitiers or the resentful, you are likely to encounter a more subtle form of resistance. It isn't that they don't understand you or are incapable of applying your teachings. In these cases counseling comes to a screeching halt because they just don't want to change. Why give up all the sympathy and mollycoddling you get from others when moping around the house gets you a pat on the head with an accompanying loving, "There, there"? And why give up your bullying anger which gets you everything you want? Being a dictator isn't half bad as long as you're dishing out the orders instead of receiving them. Naturally the conceited and grandiose person who dominates others and gets what is wanted from them is not going to take kindly to your counsel on how to control this objectionable behavior. No real change is wanted. It is small wonder that such a person will look you straight in the face and say: "Sorry, but I tried to follow your advice and it just didn't do a thing for me. Now what do you suggest?"

TELEPHONE THERAPY

Since RET is an educational process, it is perfectly possible to teach through the medium of books, tapes, lectures, and seminars. However, it can also take place over the telephone.

Out of necessity I have conducted a great many therapy sessions over the phone both within the city in which I reside and across the country. People have sought me out and wanted to come to the Quad Cities for counseling. Since long travel is time-consuming and costly, I have naturally tended to discourage it. Instead, we usually work them into my schedule like anyone else except in these cases we keep the appointment by phone.

Practically everyone finds this an acceptable method. Only about 5 percent are so uncomfortable in talking about their problems this way that they prefer not to do it at all.

Keeping appointments over the telephone makes sense also when the weather is inclement or when the client cannot get out of the house for some reason. Then, too, if your client does not show up or seems to have forgotten the appointment, you, the counselor, can easily call the person's home at the time of the appointment and suggest that you two might just as well continue the discussion now since it was scheduled.

The idea that you have to have eye-to-eye contact with your client, that you have to have a total personal involvement with your client is totally fallacious. I cannot honestly say that the therapy I have done face-to-face has necessarily been better than that which has been done over a distance of one or two thousand miles.

MAKING INTERPRETATIONS

In brief therapy it is important to give the client your ideas as soon as you formulate them. You may not always be sure of your interpretations, but that is not terribly important. When you think you have a *reasonable understanding* of why the lady behaves as she does, tell her so. If the interpretation is clearly wrong, she will let you know in her own way that it does not make sense. If she can defend her protest, you can always modify your interpretation or give her another one.

There is nothing wrong with the whole idea of trial and error in interpretations. This in itself is part of the debate process. By telling a person why he or she is doing something, and by that person's disagreeing with you, you can at least get into a conversation that can lead to further clarification until finally both of you see the dynamics more clearly.

To suggest to Mr. Williams that he has a need to punish himself by failing at his profession and that he is doing this out of a feeling of guilt over a dead brother can at least get Mr. Williams to think about the whole issue. He may come back and insist that he has worked out his guilt feelings toward his brother a long time ago and that something else is probably causing him to be self-defeating. You might then come back and suggest that he might be using his failure to gain promotions as a way of manipulating someone in his family. To this he might respond that he has wondered the same thing about spitefully trying to aggravate his ambitious wife by not moving up the managerial ladder.

This is not infrequently the way interpretations lead to deeper and deeper understanding. He is a human being and when he is wrong he can certainly acknowledge that and offer another interpretation. In fact, he will find that his interpretations get to be better and better aimed as he eliminates the unacceptable ones. If they do miss the mark, they are seldom *that* far off that he has to be humiliated or embarrassed because he did not hit the bull's eye each time.

BRINGING THE RELUCTANT CLIENT INTO COUNSELING

The important people in your client's life—spouse, parent, or relative—can often be brought into the therapeutic process to good advantage. First, advise your client that you want to see the party back home. You want the mate to come in because you need more information on your client and want another viewpoint as to what is happening in the marriage. So far you have only half of the story.

The emphasis here is to bring the reluctant mate to therapy not on a pretense that you want another person's viewpoint, but because that is actually the case. You hope, of course, that after you get into a relaxed discussion with the other half of the couple you will then be able to involve that client in any way that seems appropriate.

If this fails, you may want to write a note to the other partner to be carried by your client. Again, it can simply state that you want him or her to make an appointment because you need to understand more about the marriage so that you can help his wife or her husband.

And finally, failing this, you may want to get on the telephone and talk to the reluctant mate and express your wish directly. I find that this practically never fails and I always use it as a last resort.

THE BACKLASH

When you have persuaded one person in a marriage to make the necessary changes that the other person has been complaining about for a long time, you naturally expect the one making the complaint to be quite pleased with the changes. Sometimes this is precisely what happens, but often enough expect the opposite to happen.

I recently talked to a husband who had a number of complaints about his wife. Through my counseling she decided that if her marriage was to succeed, she was going to have to give in to him on several important points. I persuaded her to do so, and lo and behold, he came back the next week saying that he had even fewer feelings for his wife than he did before.

How to explain this phenomenon? First, the husband was irritated that the wife could change so quickly. He had been badgering her for well over a year to make those changes. I talked to her for half an hour and she went home and gave him the kind of attention and performed the sort of duties that he could not get her to do in a year's time. That bothered him.

Secondly, the fact that she turned around and became a sweetheart in a matter of a few days did not give him the full opportunity he needed to drain the hostility from his system. He still had a number of things he had to tell her and hostilities he had to express. The moment she became nice she cut off his right to tell her how nasty she had been over the whole previous year and it simply left him more frustrated than before.

Thirdly, during the time that the husband was complaining about his wife he developed a number of fantasies about how he might leave her, which other women he might take up with, and how life would be very pleasant with them. The moment she turned out to be a pleasing and loving person those dreams were shot to pieces. That too was additionally frustrating.

As a result of this observation I have found that it is

important to tell the couple I am counseling to expect the situation to deteriorate for a matter of several weeks to a month after the one party tries to improve. They are urged not to judge the status of their marriage by the fact that they are experiencing this backlash. I strongly urge them to continue with my recommendations for at least a period of three months and possibly six to see whether or not the injured party's feeling will change. Three to six months seems to be a reasonable amount of time to expect people to offer new behaviors and to see what the effect of that strategy would be. Anything less would not represent the truest picture of the dynamics between them.

ACCEPT YOURSELF AS AN EXPERT IN RATIONAL THINKING AND SANE LIVING

Because RET is a highly directive form of counseling, the client will sometimes feel that you are making pronouncements left and right as though you were King Solomon himself. In some instances you may even be accused of being conceited because you will act like a know-it-all. Every objection the client comes up with is answered with a well-rehearsed set of counter suggestions. This can be irritating to someone whose philosophy is being eroded session by session.

Though it is important to do this gently and with diplomacy, it is still important to do it. Do not back down from what you know is so. Consider yourself an expert, the teacher, the one who has studied the subject, and your client as the one who does not have your information and that's why he or she is there seeing you. If the client knew so much, why isn't he or she sitting in your chair?

You had better learn how to defend yourself when accused of conceit or you will find yourself backing down on being as assertive of your convictions as you could be. When this happened to me once in a group during which I was accused by a woman of being the most conceited person she had ever met, I told her that this simply wasn't true. She was confusing fact with opinion.

In effect what she was saying was that I thought I was so much better than everyone else because I was less disturbed than everyone in the room. I had in fact made that statement and she thought I was conceited because of it. I insisted, however, that this was not a conceited statement, it was the truth. I reported that I have never been in therapy in my life. I had never had a tranquilizer in my life. I had never seriously thought of killing myself or killing someone else. I very seldom get nervous, depressed, or worried. I am highly self-disciplined. As far as I knew there was no one in the room who had come close to that performance. So where was I wrong in saying that I was the least disturbed member of the group?

She then retorted that I didn't have to be so conceited about it. To that I replied that I was not conceited. I was simply stating a fact. It would be conceit if I had concluded that I was better than anyone in the group *because* I was less disturbed. But that's not what I had done. I had said simply that I was less disturbed and there were perfectly good reasons why that was the case. I had done a lot of studying on the subject, I practiced it every day, I preached it every day, so why shouldn't I be less disturbed? Would they seriously want to come to somebody who was *more* disturbed than they?

Conceit would have existed if I had evaluated myself better *as a person* than someone else because I was better *in some respects.* The man who makes ten times the money his neighbor earns is not ten times better as a person, only ten times better as a wage earner.

These are the kinds of experiences a counselor will encounter from time to time which will test his position as an authority. It is one on which he does not want to waver. He is the knowledgeable one and although he can sometimes learn something from his client that might expand the theory of RET, most of the time he will not. Ninety-five percent of the time he will hear objections that he has heard hundreds of times before and to which he can respond with confidence and authority.

THE PERSONALITY OF THE RET THERAPIST

Does it take a certain kind of a person to be an RET therapist? I believe it does. Not everyone in the counseling field is going to use this particular method. It calls for a style of dealing with people which is simply not compatible with every personality. I therefore think it would be important for you to study these comments and reflect upon them in some detail if you notice that you are not having much success as an RET therapist. It may be that you do not have that personality, or are not comfortable in developing that personality style which RET therapists generally possess.

First of all, we are a risk-taking group of people. We feel fairly sure about our viewpoint and we do not hesitate in most cases to offer our opinions. We know that we are taking a risk when we give advice, but we are comfortable in living with that. We don't always have to be right, and being shown that we are wrong generally does not threaten us terribly.

We take stands on issues rather than reflect endlessly on them. An RET therapist is quite likely to say to a husband that if it is all right to come home late without calling his wife then it is all right for his wife to do the same thing. We sometimes border on the opinionated, but more often we simply have strong views and do not hesitate to express them to our clients.

We also do not feel sorry for our clients. Life is tough and we accept that as part of being alive. Nor do we think that mollycoddling our clients does them much good. People want results, they don't want sympathy that makes them feel good for the moment but leaves them frustrated later on. Ours is not the soft-soaping, hand-holding technique. Ours is a straightforward, direct, and sometimes even very hard-hitting method of conversing. This does not mean that we are callous, unfeeling, or indifferent. But it does mean that we understand reality and think that a healthy respect for reality is more than dreaming or wishful thinking about life.

RET therapists usually enjoy debate. They can argue with the best of arguers and get more pleasure out of that than simply listening passively. They are a bit impatient with people's absurdities and want to push their own saner views to prevent their clients from hurting themselves. This means that RET therapists are fairly self-confident and know what they are about. Their sense of sureness comes through even though they are perfectly willing to admit that they might be wrong now or be proven wrong in the future.

RET therapists like things neat and clean. Things must make sense. They like to be reasoning persons and logical in their approach to life. They have a healthy respect for intellectualizing. Although they can be feeling persons, they are also practical and rational, and respect the rational approach over the hysterical. The experiential, as valid as that may be, is to RET therapists only a means of arriving at greater cognitive control of life.

If you possess these traits, you will probably feel comfortable as an RET therapist. If not, seek out other schools of counseling because you will probably be more effective following them than you would the RET persuasion.

DETERMINING
ORGANIC VS. FUNCTIONAL DISORDERS

When you hear of a problem and you are not at all certain whether or not it might be organic, there is a simple technique that can be helpful although it is not definitive. I immediately ask a person who tells me of an organic complaint whether there was something that happened which brought on the complaint. If the headache was accompanied by a quarrel, then I can comfortably assume that it is largely psychological in nature. If the headache came on in the middle of the day without any frustration being involved, I'm inclined to believe it might be physical.

Stomachaches, skin rashes, dizzy spells, and the like can all occur for organic or functional reasons. Unless you get a clear idea which cause applies, you might waste a lot of counseling time with a person whose stomach pains are due to problems with his career, or whose rash results from drinking coffee. If you will make the effort to look for the life stresses *prior* to the appearance of these symptoms, you can help the person. If you cannot discover those stresses, you had better refer your client to a physician.

DON'T LOSE FAITH IN YOUR THEORY

Until it is proved otherwise by powerful evidence, you can make the safe assumption that enough work has been done in the field of counseling and with RET that you can certainly have great faith in it. For example, if a client tells you that he is not thinking of anything just before he gets depressed, do not accept that. The RET theory states that the depression is preceded by certain irrational thoughts and there is no reason why this will not apply in this case. You may want to keep an open mind about exceptions because it is possible that your client is a hypoglycemic or has other chemical imbalances that could bring on depression. But until you get such evidence, have faith in your theory first and use it to back up your statements.

Only recently I was talking to a teenager who was giving his family one bad time. I pointed out to him that he was making himself upset because he either wanted attention and affection, or because he wanted to punish his parents, demonstrate his power, or because he wanted to remain infantile. He denied these goals categorically but could not offer any other reason for his behavior. I felt fairly sure that he was not reacting in an irrational way because of some physical reason so I simply relied upon my faith in RET. I insisted that he had to have frustrating feelings about one of those four commonly experienced adolescent problems. Again he refused to accept my interpretation and again I insisted that I was right. After a few moments of silence he hesitantly offered the suggestion that of the four it sounded to him like his desire for recognition and attention was the most likely interpretation. At that point he began to answer every one of my questions about his need for attention in the affirmative. During the next fifteen minutes I was absolutely convinced that his soiling his pants, stealing, and rebelliousness were his desperate measures to get the attention of his family.

I must confess, however, that the boy had me wondering for a while. One can have blind faith and this is one of those dangers we fall into when we become too smug or overly confident and do not allow for new insights. Don't be 100 percent sure, but why not 90 percent? If you aren't that certain, do not hesitate to refer the client to other professionals for further study. Family physicians, optometrists, neurologists, etc., are only several of the resources open to us in moments of doubt.

DON'T BE AN OTHER-PITIER

Too close an identification with your client's problems can get you so disturbed that in short order your own emotional life will be disturbed. This tendency to identify too closely with people we want to help has long been recognized and is something that is looked for closely in graduate training. Those people who grieve and weep over everybody's aches and sorrows either are trained to overcome this tendency or are asked to change career goals. Unfortunately, like the phoenix, this human tendency arises afresh from time to time as we encounter human miseries in our practice that are new to us. It is at that point that we are likely to become upset over the injustices of the world and the huge, crushing hurts to which our people are exposed. Our thoughts can be with them night and day if we but let them.

That is no way to be a brief therapist. Unless you can shut your mind to your client's enormous frustration when the client leaves your room just as readily as you shut the door, you are in trouble. The trick is to be able to listen and then set aside the previous client's troubles while you give your full and fresh attention to the next. And if you ever expect to have a private practice that will include ten to sixteen clients a day, you had better learn this task well. One of the best ways to handle this problem is to accept the rational idea that *one does not have to be disturbed over other people's problems and disturbances.* Get hold of that idea securely, think it through in great depth, and accept it as a wonderfully sane piece of advice. This does not mean you have to be underconcerned, but it does not mean you have to be over-concerned either. Merely being concerned, caring, and trying to be your brother's keeper, these are all perfectly sane atti-tudes to take. They show that you care about others and that you are exerting your energies and efforts in their behalf. But to become disturbed or to be uncaring *at all* is unworthy of you as a counselor. You will know immediately when you are overconcerned rather than just concerned by the fact that you will feel uncomfortable. You will be depressed over your client, angry against somebody who has mistreated him, or nervous that something bad may happen to him. When you begin to feel like that *you are too involved.* Stop pitying people and you will bring yourself back on the right track.

THE CLIENT WHO WILL NOT TALK

What is more exasperating and taxing than a client who comes in repeatedly, faithfully, seems to be well motivated, sits down, and doesn't say a word? Counselors really earn their keep when they run up against one of these enigmas, and I have had my share of them.

I can do one of two things in dealing with clients who will not talk. Either I lay down the law and tell them they have to talk up or end therapy, or I decide to continue counseling because the client is fragile and needs the relationship desper-ately. I then do not press for termination or for speech but let them come and sit as long as they want. I try to talk about anything meaningful, to give a lecture on psychology, to talk about those particular emotions I think they are suffering from, and to give them insight into their condition even though they never once opened their mouths. It is perfectly possible for some people to learn by listening even though they seem not to be actively engaged. The day may come when they do open up and you will be surprised at how much they have absorbed. If they do not eventually communicate with you, they may terminate anyway, and whether they have gained or not is their responsibility. You have done your best when you have talked yourself blue in the face and been a patient and tolerant counselor. What more can anyone ask?

WHEN THE COUNSELOR REMAINS SILENT

I have made the point repeatedly that the RET brand of counseling is a form of education and that the client is actually a student who has come to learn about psychology from the teacher who is the counselor.

However, there are some instances when this is not true. As with all forms of therapy, a type of client exists who does not want counseling in the strict sense of the word. Mr. Berry, for example, wants ventilation. He comes in filled with the story that he has to unburden and whether he is looking for sympathy or just catharsis, the point remains that he is not interested in your views, your interpretations, or your advice. He simply wants an ear to talk to, a shoulder to lean on, a sympathetic nod, a smile and a pat on the back as he leaves the room. His mission is complete when he has told you of some sad event, some injustice, or a rehearsal of his unhappy life. People such as Mr. Berry want friendship, not instruction. To interrupt this recitation is to deny them the benefits for which they came.

When I sense that I am encountering a person who has the weight of the world on his chest and simply wants someone to talk to so that he can get relief from his burden, I usually accept the situation as given and lean back in my chair and remain silent with the exception of an "I see" or give him a Rogerian nod. At the end of half an hour or an hour he leaves feeling much better and I feel more rested.

Has he gained from this encounter? Yes and no. He feels better, to be sure. His resentments have been expressed, his hurts have been aired, his grievances have been reviewed, and the bitter feelings have momentarily been dissipated. But *is* he better? I think not. He has gotten an aspirin for a headache when he could have been given instructions on how to avoid one. He has emptied himself of bad feelings but has not learned how to avoid future bad feelings. However, that was his choice. He was not ready for education and until he is more open to the instruction process he will go from event to event feeling better for brief periods of time until the next buildup.

WHEN YOU TANGO ALONE

It is high time that we got over the idea that it takes two to tango. I think this is a serious mistake, because we sometimes fail to realize that one partner or member of the family can be simply a pain in the neck and that other people, out of defense, react against that person.

Why isn't it possible for a perfectly well adjusted, easygoing, and quite mature person to be thrown into a relationship with a neurotic who badgers him or her in a million ways? Why is it wrong for the mature person to fight back and assert himself or herself aggressively against this thoughtless individual? Are we seriously to believe that both of them are contributing equally to the problem? I think not. One person can be so disturbed in a relationship as to invite defensive behavior from everyone else, and if that one person would straighten out, the others would get along quite nicely.

Family therapy continually makes the point that a problem exists only within the matrix of the family and that it cannot exist by itself. By why can't it? A perfectly well adjusted couple who gave birth to an autistic child are not going to have a miserable family life because they suddenly turn into nitwits. The family life becomes disrupted because of that one single individual who is simply impossible to handle. People can, all by themselves, cause all kinds of havoc.

These people tango by themselves. True, the others will often respond with anger or depression, but that hardly means that they are *responsible* for what they are defending themselves against. If a bully comes up to you and starts to fight, you may have to wind up socking him and rolling on the ground with him in order to defend yourself. But you are doing so in self-defense, not because you have a neurotic problem equal to his. And I think this is precisely what happens in many other relationships which we too often thought of as being brought about by the irresponsible behavior of both parties when it was mainly the irresponsible behavior on the part of the *one* very disturbed person.

DON'T DISCOURAGE MILD DEGREES OF DISTURBANCE

Books on self-help psychology have rightly been criticized for trying to present an image of mental health which is unrealistic. The view has been put forth that a person is mentally healthy only when feeling no guilt, no depression, no anger, no anxiety, and so on. This is obviously an unrealistic view of human nature.

There are, in fact, *merits* to mild emotional disturbances. For example, unless someone has a twinge of guilt, there is nothing to tell the person that the act just committed is wrong. To feel enormously guilty over an act and to become immobilized over it is another matter.

Unless a person feels some annoyance, a touch of anger, how can the person know that the act just experienced was one that had better be protested? The same can be said for fear. Fear and tension of a mild sort can make a person alert to present dangers, can heighten the senses so that competitive tasks or dangerous skills can be performed with greater competence. The person who is blasé is in serious trouble because he or she does not prepare for obvious dangers and does not sharpen wits and skills to a fine edge against those who are somewhat more keyed up.

In short, to become mildly disturbed is not all bad and it is about time that we let people feel comfortable with these neurotic but very mild reactions. In the final analysis we are truly interested in preventing the self-defeating emotional disturbances, those which last for a painful length of time or which seriously disrupt productivity or interpersonal relationships. It is only then that our pursuit of happiness and our inner sense of stability is truly disrupted. The milder emotional reactions can be positive experiences and need not be thrown out in the same bath water that we throw out when we get rid of the more serious emotional disturbances.

THE MOST IMPORTANT QUESTION

In brief therapy the repeated task of the counselor is to get the clients to understand what they are saying to themselves and then have them challenge the irrationalities. In practice the most frequent and important question that the counselor repeatedly asks the client is, "What did you tell yourself just before you became upset?" This statement can be followed with an elaboration once in a while to the effect: "If you will recall or jot down for me those times when you are upset and try to remember what you said to yourself immediately before you became upset, I will show you which of those thoughts were irrational and which were rational. And I will show you why they are irrational and how to combat them."

The counselor can confidentially expand even that theme and say: "No matter what situation you give me I will show you in every case precisely how you upset yourself if you will give me some idea as to what your thoughts were at that time. And I will show you in every case precisely how you can talk yourself out of the disturbance caused by your wrong thinking."

This may sound grandiose, but it is not. When RET counselors learn what is going on in the heads of the clients they can indeed tell them how their disturbance was created and what they had better do to undo it. Whether the clients will diligently do their homework remains up to them. These resistances often spring from other irrational ideas which can be approached by the counselor with the question, "What are you telling yourself just before you avoid the homework?" And so it goes.

ALWAYS ENCOURAGE SELF-DEBATE

In all counseling, one task is more critical than any other. It is self-debate. Throughout your counseling it is practically always critical that you keep the client oriented toward questioning, challenging, and debating with himself over his irrational ideas. If Mr. Miller is not moving in the direction that he wants to proceed, it means that he is still saying one or more irrational things to himself and these can only be removed and conquered by his thinking about them very seriously and debating them vigorously. Debate, debate, debate.

One of the more picturesque ways I sometimes describe the process to the client is to suggest to him that he has, figuratively speaking, two tape recorders in his head. On one recorder there are a whole string of irrational ideas while on the other recorder there are many rational ideas. His problem is that he listens to the irrational ideas because he has the volume on that machine turned up much louder than on the rational machine. I urge him to listen more carefully to the voice of reason, to counter every irrational statement with a rational statement whether he believes it or not. It is my contention that before one can believe an idea, it has to at least reside in the mental framework of the person who is to adopt it. Unless it is available for inspection, it cannot be accepted. That is why it is so important for him to at least say these rational ideas to himself, out loud if necessary. He begins to hear them, to become familiar with them, to feel comfortable with them. And only after he continually says them over to himself a number of times can he begin to allow himself perhaps to see how sensible they actually are.

If the brief counselor will make more of an effort to emphasize the self-debate process, he will find that his improvement rate will go up.

When the woman client turns to you and says, "I did debate with myself," you can only encourage her to double the amount of debating she did. In all likelihood she may have spent no more than thirty seconds trying to think her way out of her dilemma. Thirty seconds is not enough. Thirty minutes may not be enough. She may want to return to her irrational thoughts throughout an entire day and continually resist many times throughout the day. Or she may want to stay with the debate on a continuous basis for an hour or two.

We come down to the easily observed psychological fact that when people seriously and vigorously question their neurotic philosophies great changes follow. That self-debate is the crucial factor. Remember, Ellis pointed out that we had better realize that *(a)* emotional disturbances come from our thoughts, *(b)* debating these irrational philosophies until we no longer believe them is the second critical step, and *(c)* nothing else is necessary.

THERAPIST: You were saying you were doing a little better but you had a bad time. Can you explain to me why you had a bad time?

WIFE: I keep piling things on myself. I keep saying garbage to myself, like thinking I'm bad because I ignored the baby.

T: Now when did this happen the last time?

W: It was on Tuesday. It was a bad day, Tuesday. I just felt crummy about not having enough of an intellectual challenge. I don't know what really starts it. Sometimes I get up in the morning feeling that way. But then I keep talking to myself and saying how I'm a rotten mother and Timmy is there and wants me to play and I'll play with him and then I'll look around the house and the house is a mess. I'm a rotten housekeeper. I just keep piling it on myself.

T: Life is not challenging enough and you want to get back to the professional world?

W: Yes. That was my major thought that day. I was in the wrong place at the wrong time with the wrong people.

HUSBAND: I think it was when we went out for tacos.

W: I was talking to myself in the afternoon. I think I was in a pretty good mood, a better mood when you got home.

H: I do too. I think you were facing it better. You were kind of accepting it.

W: I was catching myself by the afternoon. I think when we

were at the taco place that's when it really came to a head but by afternoon I was saying to myself: "You're just having a bad day. It doesn't mean that you've made a bad decision or you've had eight years of bad days." I was just having a bad day. I was tired. When I finally identified it and nailed it down, "This is a bad day," I realized my whole life wasn't bad, that I'm not bad. I'm starting to do what you suggested to separate the acts from the person. And because I was having a bad day because I was choosing to ignore my child didn't mean I was a crummy person.

T: Right.

W: It takes a lot of energy especially when you're down and you're vulnerable and you're tired and you're out of energy. You need the energy to deal with the garbage.

T: How much time do you think you took to debate with yourself and to analyze your irrational thoughts, and to talk yourself back into some sensible position? How long did that take?

W: I don't know. I lay down when Timmy did and took a two-hour nap. Then I was ready to get up and that's when the wheels started turning in the other direction.

T: Then you were in a better frame of mind and could begin to make yourself think more rationally after you got a little rest?

W: Yes. I had the energy to deal with it.

T: Well, that worked well on that day when you needed the rest. But can you see also that on other days you weren't especially tired and you were still thinking in a very upsetting way? And going to bed might not have helped very much at all?

W: Right.

T: At those times what are the things that you think you had better do more of?

W: Just talking to myself in a rational, reasonable way.

T: Right.

W: I think this day that I was talking about when I was tired I don't think I was physically *that* tired. I think I was mentally exhausted from what I was telling myself. Actually I ache today and I am more tired but my head's on right today.

T: It is very important for you to spend much more time debating and challenging and analyzing all of the irrational things that you are telling yourself. One task more than any other is the biggest stumbling block. People give themselves nonsense to think about and then they leave it there. If somebody told you your car has just turned into a pumpkin, you'd immediately question that. You'd think about it and immediately you'd arrive at a number of conclusions, "Well, that's interesting," or "You're crazy," or something like that. But when we say those things to ourselves we just leave it there. We just say, "Period." Therefore we go around all day long thinking that we're bad, or that our car is turning into a pumpkin, or that we've got the most miserable lives in the whole world. None of that is actually true. Most of us live decent lives compared to the people around the world, and we are just always getting upset about what we have.

W: I had a woman call me that really had problems. I can see where she is feeding irrational stuff to herself and I can pick it out and say to myself, "Why is she believing all this and living it?" I even question what other mixed-up people are saying to themselves. But somehow we feed it to ourselves like it was Rice Krispies. It is just amazing to me how I can. I'm a good listener. People come to me with problems and I'm good at listening, and yet here I am. I can't do it for myself.

T: That's right. It's about time you did the same thing and listened to what you're saying and really thought about it. I want you to take those ideas you have and put them under a microscope and say: "Now let me study this carefully. I have just written a script for myself, if you will, and it says certain things. Now I am going to think about this. It's like a play I have written for myself. I've written a description of myself. Here it is in manuscript form. I'm going to sit down in a nice easy chair and I am going to examine this thing word for word." And then see if it is true. And if it isn't, then take a pencil and cross it off and write another. So think about these things and I can practically guarantee you that you've got to come out of most of your disturbances. When you don't overcome these painful and disturbing emotional problems it can usually be traced to that one fault. You haven't done your homework. You haven't thought it through enough. You have said something false to yourself and you haven't spent enough time seeing the flaws in what you have just said.

LOVE THOSE CLIENTS

Zen philosophy (Murphy and White, 1978) has been telling us for a long time that we gain a greater advantage by becoming one with the problem we are dealing with rather than by considering it as an enemy. In tennis, for example, an attitude that considers the ball as a loving object, as a friendly missile coming toward you that you will gladly return across the net to a particular point, makes your control over that ball all the better. To consider the ball as an irritation, as something that must be smashed to downgrade your opponent, causes you to lose control over the ball.

Clients can be seen in the same light. They are not there to vex you. They are not there to aggravate you. They are there to stimulate you, to enrich your life, to broaden your horizons. You welcome them into your office even if they behave badly. This too can be educational. It is a human experience and as such falls within your purview of understanding. Your clients are enormously important to you because they give you purpose. They are persons to appreciate, to help, to care for. The less you fight them, the farther you can move together.

Love those clients! It is through them that you can learn about yourself. Clients and their experiences, errors, arrogance, rudeness, laziness, are all elements in your own education. Clients are the key to your therapeutic success. Rejoice and be glad you have them.

References

Adler, Alfred
  1965. *Superiority and Social Interest: A Collection of Later Writings.* Ed. by Heinz L. Ansbacher and Rowena R. Ansbacher. Northwestern University Press.
Alexander, Franz, and Ross, Helen
  1952. *Dynamic Psychiatry.* University of Chicago Press.
Anderson, Camilla M.
  1966. "Depression and Suicide Reassessed," *Journal of American Women's Association,* 1964, Vol. 19. Reprinted in *Rational Living,* Vol. 1, No. 2, pp. 31–36.
Arieti, Silvano, ed.
  1959. *American Handbook of Psychiatry.* 3 vols. (Vols. 1 and 2, 1959; Vol. 3, 1966). Basic Books.
Bakan, C.
  1962. "Suicide and the Method of Introspection," *The Journal of Existential Psychiatry,* Vol. 2, No. 7, pp. 313–322.
Beck, Aaron T.
  1963. "Thinking and Depression," *Archives of General Psychiatry,* Vol. 9, pp. 324–333.
  1967. *Depression: Clinical, Experimental, and Theoretical Aspects.* Paul B. Hoeber.
Block, J., and Christiansen, B.
  1966. "A Test of Hendin's Hypothesis Relating Suicide in Scandinavia to Child-rearing Orientations," *Scandinavian Journal of Psychology,* Vol. 7, pp. 267–288.
Bychowski, Gustav
  1968. *Evil in Man.* Grune & Stratton.

Dreikurs, Rudolf
  1964. and Soltz, Vicki. *Children: The Challenge.* Meredith Press.
  1968. *Psychology in the Classroom.* 2d ed. Harper & Row.
Durant, Will, and Durant, Ariel
  1963. *The Story of Civilization,* Vol. VIII: *The Age of Louis XIV.* Simon & Schuster.
Ellis, Albert
  1957. *How to Live with a Neurotic.* Crown Publishers.
  1961. and Harper, Robert A. *A Guide to Rational Living.* Prentice-Hall.
  1962. *Reason and Emotion in Psychotherapy.* Lyle Stuart.
  1963. "Toward a More Precise Definition of 'Emotional' and 'Intellectual' Insight," *Psychological Reports,* 13, pp. 125–126.
  1966. and others. *How to Prevent Your Child from Becoming a Neurotic Adult.* Crown Publishers.
  1969. "Teaching Emotional Education in the Classroom," *School Health Review,* November, pp. 10–13.
  1971. and Gullo, John M. *Murder and Assassination.* Lyle Stuart.
  1972. *Executive Leadership: A Rational Approach.* Citadel Press.
  1973. *Humanistic Psychotherapy: The Rational-Emotive Approach.* Julian Press.
Epictetus
  1899. *The Works of Epictetus.* Tr. by Thomas W. Higginson. Little, Brown & Co.
Farberow, Norman L., and Shneidman, Edwin S., eds.
  1961. *The Cry for Help.* McGraw-Hill.
Fischer, William F.
  1970. *Theories of Anxiety.* Harper & Row.
Freud, Sigmund
  1935. *The Psychopathology of Everyday Life.* Tr. by A. A. Brill. London: Ernest Benn.
  1938. *The Basic Writings of Sigmund Freud.* Tr. and ed. by A. A. Brill. Modern Library.
  1945. *The Psychoanalytic Theory of Neurosis.* W. W. Norton & Co.
Glasser, William
  1969. *Schools Without Failure.* Harper & Row.

Hadas, Moses, ed.
1962. *Essential Works of Stoicism.* Bantam Books.
Hall, Calvin S., and Lindzey, Gardner
1970. *Theories of Personality.* 2d ed. John Wiley & Sons.
Hauck, Paul A.
1967. *The Rational Management of Children.* 2d rev. ed. Libra Publishers, 1972.
1972. *Reason in Pastoral Counseling.* Westminster Press.
1973. *Overcoming Depression.* Westminster Press.
1974. *Overcoming Frustration and Anger.* Westminster Press.
1975. and Kean, Edmund S., M.D. *Marriage and the Memo Method.* Westminster Press.
1975. *Overcoming Worry and Fear.* Westminster Press.
1976. *How to Do What You Want to Do: The Art of Self-Discipline.* Westminster Press.
1977. *Marriage Is a Loving Business.* Westminster Press.
1979. *How to Stand Up for Yourself.* Westminster Press.
Hurlock, Elizabeth B.
1973. *Adolescent Development.* 4th ed. McGraw-Hill.
Kisker, George W.
1972. *The Disorganized Personality.* 2d ed. McGraw-Hill.
Mahoney, Michael J., and Thoresen, Carl E.
1974. *Self-Control: Power to the Person.* Brooks/Cole Publishing Co.
Marcus Aurelius
1900. *The Thoughts of the Emperor Marcus Aurelius Antonius.* Little, Brown & Co.
Marx, Melvin H., ed.
1970. *Learning: Theories.* Macmillan Co.
Maultsby, Maxie C., Jr.
1975. *Help Yourself to Happiness Through Rational Self-Counseling.* Institute for Rational Living.
Meichenbaum, Donald H.
1977. *Cognitive-Behavior Modification.* Plenum Publishing Corp.
Mintz, R.
1961. "Psychotherapy of the Suicidal Patient," *American Journal of Psychotherapy,* Vol. 15, No. 3, pp. 348–367 (a).
Murphy, Michael, and White, Rhea
1978. *The Psychic Side of Sports.* Addison-Wesley Publishing Co.

Nardi, T. J.
  1979. "The Use of Psychodrama in RET," *Rational Living,* Vol.
  14, No. 1 (Spring), pp. 35–38.
Phillips, E. Lakin, and Wiener, Daniel N.
  1972. *Discipline, Achievement, and Mental Health.* 2d ed. Prentice-Hall.
Robins, Lee N.
  1966. *Deviant Children Grown Up.* Williams & Wilkins Co.
Rogers, Carl R.
  1951. *Client-centered Therapy.* Houghton Mifflin Co.
  1961. *On Becoming a Person.* Houghton Mifflin Co.
Solzhenitsyn, Aleksandr I.
  1975. *The Gulag Archipelago, Two.* Harper & Row.
Szasz, Thomas S.
  1961. *The Myth of Mental Illness.* Harper & Brothers.
Watson, David L., and Tharp, Roland G.
  1972. *Self-directed Behavior.* Brooks/Cole Publishing Co.
Zax, Melvin, and Cowen, Emory L.
  1972. *Abnormal Psychology: Changing Conceptions.* Holt, Rine-
  hart & Winston.